Wonder, Wisdom and War
Essays on early Ireland

Wonder, Wisdom and War

Essays on early Ireland

Brendan Halligan

www.scathánpress.com

Wonder, Wisdom and War – Essays on early Ireland
First Edition, Published by:
Scáthán Press
Dublin, Ireland

Trade and order inquiries to:
editor@brendanhalligan.com
www.brendanhalligan.com

© Brendan Halligan, 2015

ISBN: 978-0-9927948-2-8

This book is sold subject to the condition that it shall not, by way of trade or otherwise, be lent, resold, hired out, digitally reproduced or otherwise circulated without the publisher's prior consent in any form of binding, cover or digital format other than that in which it is published and without a similar condition being imposed on the subsequent purchaser.

Book design by Cyberscribe.ie
Cover pic: © Helena Mulkerns

Contents

About the Author		9
Preface		11
Chapter 1:	Great Exhaltation: the beginnings of writing in Old Irish	15
Chapter 2:	Hierarchical, Inegalitarian, Aristrocratic: Status in early Irish society	47
Chapter 3:	Advice from a princely in-law: the wisdom texts in Old Irish	75
Chapter 4:	A Window on the Iron age: the controversary over the dating of The Ulster Cycle	125
Bibliography		185

About the Author

Known today as a man of politics, an economist and current Chairman of the Institute of International and European Affairs (IIEA), Brendan Halligan worked in the public sector before entering politics in 1967, when he became General-Secretary of the Irish Labour Party.

During his political career, he served as a member of the Irish Senate (1973) an elected member of the Irish Dáil (parliament) and a Member of the European Parliament. He founded the Institute of International and European Affairs (IIEA), was director of his own firm, Consultants in Public Affairs (CIPA), from 1985 to 2014 and is a member of the Board of Mainstream Renewable Power.

Brendan Halligan holds a Masters in Economics from University College Dublin and has written extensively about economics and politics. He is a keen scholar and speaker of the Irish language, and was an Adjunct Professor in European Integration at the University of Limerick. In 2010, he was granted an Honorary Degree of Doctor of Literature by University College Dublin.

He studied Early Irish history, language and culture in Trinity College, Dublin as a mature student, and has a particular interest in early Irish poetry and the sagas, especially the *Táin Bó Cuailgna*.

Preface

These four essays on early Irish society and Old Irish were written as part of my undergraduate studies in Trinity College Dublin during the period from 2001 to 2003. I had wanted to do something completely new on reaching the retirement age of sixty-five and decided to study Old Irish – a long held ambition. I duly enrolled in TCD as an undergraduate and started on the BA in October 2001.

Naturally, I bit off more than I could chew. I never sat for the degree, but I did enjoy three years studying with an inspiring set of professors and lecturers. Pride of place went to Professor Damian McManus who lectured me in both Old and Modern Irish, but who specialised in teaching Old Irish. I emphasise 'teaching' because he was a gifted teacher, which was just as well since learning Old Irish is one of the toughest challenges that could face any student, however willing.

It is, to put it mildly, a difficult field of study but he helped a small group of students to develop an expertise in our ancestral language. Some persevered to the end, and one even became an academic in the subject.

This is as far as I got and the essays presented here were written during the first two years of the course, on topics set by the lecturers. Of necessity, the style is academic, which means it is somewhat turgid. I hope, nevertheless, that the content proves to be of some value to those interested in Irish history and culture, and that the essays may cast some light on early Irish society.

If they encourage anybody to search for more information on either early Irish culture or Old Irish as a language then I'll be sufficiently rewarded.

Brendan Halligan
Dublin
01 September 2015

Wonder, Wisdom and War:
Essays on early Ireland

Chapter 1

Great Exhaltation:

the beginnings of writing in old Irish

Summary

The essay title is sufficiently broad to be interpreted in a number of ways. It could relate exclusively to the act or art of writing, or to the content of what was written at the beginnings of Old Irish. Equally, it could be taken as a combination of both. Despite the obvious complexity of this latter approach, it is the definition of writing used throughout this essay. And, to fill out the interpretation of the title, Old Irish is taken as the vernacular language from ad 600 to ad 900, approximately.

Consequently, the essay is structured around the following themes:

1. *evidence for literacy in pre-Christian Ireland;*
2. *the impact of Christianity;*
3. *literacy in medieval Ireland;*
4. *the Irish literary tradition;*
5. *the use of the vernacular during this period;*
6. *the sources of Old Irish literature;*
7. *its antiquity; content; and diversity; and,*
8. *finally, a brief résumé of the various genres of Old Irish literature.*

Given the wide panorama of issues to be addressed, the treatment is, of necessity, more attenuated than the individual topics deserve. The main thesis in this essay is that the emergence of a vernacular literature was, to quote Carney (1969), something of a miracle.

This development went against the grain of medieval European society and can only be accounted for by the astonishing culture and self-confidence of the Irish learned class, who rapidly absorbed Latin literacy, adapted it to the vernacular tradition and, out of this amalgam, produced the most diverse and sophisticated literature of the period. It is argued that the greatest contribution of Old Irish to European culture is the imaginative literature contained in the sagas and poetry, and its most lasting impact on the Irish people are the histories which shaped the communal sense of self-identity down to the present.

Throughout the essay reference is made to the sources of Old Irish and their rediscovery in the nineteenth century, a story which may reasonably be described as a saga in itself..

Introduction

Virtually all authorities on the subject of early Irish literature agree, even if they agree on little else, that it is unique in a number of respects, such as its antiquity, diversity, continuity and content. It is generally accepted that it came into being about ad 600 (Carney 1969: 160).

That it did so in the face of the dominant Latin culture, Carney describes as 'a sort of miracle', and this raises the intriguing question as to whether pre-Christian Ireland was itself literate and thus managed to subsume Latin orthography and literary forms into an already existing literary tradition and, out of a dynamic fusion of the two, succeed in creating a literature which has had a continuous run to the present day (*ibid*.).

Breatnach reminds us that we have no direct evidence for the pre-literate period in Ireland and that reliance on the classical authors is no substitute (1996: 76). There may, however, be indirect evidence in the form of Ogam inscriptions on stone. Stevenson contends that literacy in Ireland 'preceded the establishment of Christianity ... possibly by centuries' (1989: 148) and justifies this belief by reference to commercial contact with the Roman world: 'throughout the Roman period Ireland was not a completely isolated island' (132), a point of reference with which McManus agrees (1991: 41). Stevenson refers to a group of loan-words from Latin into Irish which seem to reflect 'contact in the fifth century, or earlier' (1989: 131).

By way of corroboration of this pre-Christian literacy Stevenson claims that 'the ogams represent independent

Irish attempts to come to grips with the phonesis of the Irish language' (1989:144). The orthographic system of the ogam inscriptions confirms that the Irish were familiar with the Latin alphabet prior to the advent of Christianity and spelled Irish 'in line with Latin orthographic conventions' (*ibid.*). As McManus has demonstrated, there was 'no breach between the Ogam and manuscript traditions' (1991: 57), and he reminds us that 'the very act of writing implies a convention of one kind or another' (80).

It would seem that the general thesis of literacy in pre-Christian Ireland has some merit and could be used to explain how Christian Ireland produced a sophisticated literature so rapidly. This can be inferred, to put it no stronger, from McManus when he claims that 'the later monument Ogamists and the early scribes ... must have been one and the same people' (1986: 13). The evidence of overlapping and continuity between the two traditions cannot be ignored (Ó Cathasaigh, 1996: 60) and, if the evidence is accepted, then these 'oldest documents of all in the Irish language' (McCone 1996a: 16) could provide the clue to the conundrum of how Irish literacy and literature appeared to spring up so spontaneously after the advent of Christianity. Otherwise we are left without any credible sociological explanation for Carney's 'miracle'.

McManus, in what is now the standard work on Ogam, contends there is a possibility, and he puts it no stronger, that some of the inscriptions may belong to the fourth century ad. He adds that the creation of an alphabet precedes its use as a vehicle for writing by approximately one to two centuries. If so, then the third or fourth century ad would be the likely date for the creation of Ogam; and this possibility takes on force since it is 'certainly true that by the monument period the alphabet and a conventional orthography were well established throughout the country' (1991: 40).

Without wishing to place greater stress on these words than they might bear, they at least raise the possibility that literacy preceded what is conventionally taken as the date for the advent of Christianity in Ireland. It could, for example, have arrived with earlier missionaries or have been imported into small Christian communities already present on the island, such as appear to have existed in the Munster region.

It is disappointing that this question has not been more fully explored. At face value it seems difficult to accept that literacy and a sophisticated literature should emerge *ex nihilo*, with only the arrival of organised Christianity to account for both phenomena. This apparent lacuna is all the more surprising when one considers the sheer complexity of committing a spoken language to paper in terms of, to take but three key examples, phonetic transcription, orthography and a standardised grammar. Given that the Irish language presented problems for which Latin provided few models, such as initial mutations, and that Old Irish grammar was so complex, the challenge to native scholarship was, quite literally, staggering in its complexity.

That the scholars should have succeeded to the point of creating a standardised literary language within two centuries, as the evidence suggests, is testimony either to a pre-Christian literacy, which had already begun to solve these problems, or to a pre-existing learned class with a unique capacity for cultural assimilation and innovation. What could have been a threat was turned into an opportunity – with astonishing results. For that reason it is appropriate to examine the impact of Christianity on pagan Ireland.

The impact of Christianity

With the arrival of Christianity there was 'a real danger that the new Latin learning might have driven out the vernacular tradition altogether, as happened very largely in continental Germanic literature' (Byrne 1984: xvi). That this did not happen in Ireland is self-evident, but the reasons for the 'cross fertilisation of clerical and lay expertise' (Stevenson 1989: 163) which led to this outcome are hotly contested by scholars. All would agree, at least, that 'since Christianity is a religion of the Book, the early Christian communities must have had scholars among them who were literate in Latin' (Ó Cathasaigh 1996: 59), and few would contest that the pagan society they encountered had a learned class, known later as the *filid*.

While there are understandable disputes about the pace of christianisation, and somewhat scanty explanations for the relatively early demise of the pagan priesthood, the Druids, there seems to be broad agreement that from the beginning of the Christian period 'a more or less unitary learned class amalgamating pre-Christian learning with the new importation' was gradually created (Stevenson 1989: 128).

She argues that it was members of the learned classes who became the new Christian elite, and the result was 'a fusion and identification of interests' (1989: 160).

Consequent upon 'the Church's generally relaxed attitude to the society it served', the most unusual aspect of native culture in a christianised Ireland was the accommodation between them (*ibid.*).

The outcome, according to Ó Corráin (see Ó Cathasaigh 1996: 60), was the emergence of a unified 'mandarin class of literati who ranged over the whole of learning from scriptural exegesis, canon law and computistics to inherited native law, legend and genealogy'. This thesis that Christian Latin learning and native learning had coalesced in Ireland by the sixth century ad is supported by Ó Cathasaigh (*ibid.*), although with some reservations about Ó Corráin's methodology, but is disputed by MacCana (see Ó Cathasaigh 1996, 61), who believes there was a disparity between the two classes, as evidenced by the annals in the pre-Norman period.

This difference in interpretation has been exhaustively explored by McCone, who points out that 'early Christian Ireland would ... have been quite abnormal by medieval western European standards if literacy in Latin or the vernacular had existed there on any scale outside the sphere of her monasteries and their alumni' (1990: 1). He dismisses the 'romantic native dualism' (21) theory in favour of a more complex social model in which the Irish medieval literati produced 'the thoroughly integrated hybrid medium in which all extant early Irish literature, history and mythology seems to be rooted' (79).

McCone's concern, following in the footsteps of Carney (1955: 321), is with the Christian influence inherent in the content of the literature, and the sagas in particular, as the title of his book clearly indicates (1990).

But it is possible to step outside this vigorous controversy and identify the common ground on which the contest takes place. Irrespective of whether there was one or two learned classes following the advent of Christianity in Ireland, and irrespective, furthermore, of the Church's role as either a patron or a ruthless reshaper of the pagan tradition, the fact is that the vernacular survived the impact of Christianity. That it was modified, informed and recast by Christianity is beyond question; that it survived is beyond dispute. And that, as Byrne remarked, might not have happened. It was the uniqueness of Irish society in terms of its history and culture that led to an outcome that can only be described as *sui generis*. Perhaps, says Nagy, the most important result of this alliance (however it was configured politically and socially) 'between native knower/performer and ecclesiastic was the creation of a literature in both Latin and Irish' (1997: 9).

Nagy's observation is particularly helpful in that it states the obvious, that most elusive of phenomena. Christianity produced, or helped to create, a literature in two languages. This was fortuitous for our knowledge of Old Irish, as will be confirmed in a later section of this essay. As the outcome of what contemporary historians would describe as the clash of cultures it was remarkable in that it departed from the European norm, as Byrne has observed.

The result was a society in which the learned class was bilingual; indeed bilingualism became the litmus-test of learning. Nagy's commentary, therefore, helps us come to an understanding of the society that began writing (or to write in a new form) in Irish. Bilingualism in a mono-ethnic culture is not uncommon, but when used for literary purposes, as distinct from commercial or conventional communication, it is generally an index of high culture. Nagy is right in defining Christianity's main cultural impact in Ireland in terms of the literature it inspired, aside, of course, from the change in religious beliefs it introduced.

Literacy in medieval Ireland

Nagy's insight into literacy in medieval Ireland was doubtlessly based on the work of earlier scholars. For example, Carney says that literacy in medieval Ireland was 'more widely spread than in any other European country' (1969: 169). We can be sure that there was some degree of Latin literacy in the early-fifth century, even though the earliest extant manuscripts are probably no earlier than the end of the sixth century (Ó Cathasaigh 1996: 59). Literacy in the vernacular was achieved at a relatively early date, as the discussion above on Ogam suggested, and the precise dating is immaterial to the claim that vernacular literacy existed in Ireland at least by the latter part of the sixth century. Binchy, for example, believes that the Latin alphabet 'seeped into the native law schools somewhere in the sixth century' (1961: 12); an important example of the prevalence of literacy in view of the centrality of law to the then Irish social system.

One index for measuring the breadth and depth of literacy in medieval society is the confidence with which the scribes approach the actual craft of writing itself.

By this standard it would appear that literacy was well entrenched in Ireland at an even earlier date, possibly by the beginning of the sixth century, as the extant manuscripts seem to testify. 'The hands of all these ancient books', notes Stevenson, 'are practiced and confident. They confirm the impression given by the earliest Hiberno-Latin authors that literacy was well established in the religious centres by 600' (1989: 153).

If it was well established by that time, then it must have been in gestation for two generations or more before then. Furthermore, she claims that in the following half century it is clear that book promotion was quite extensive, further evidence of a developed high culture that would have been maturing over a number of generations. More importantly for the purposes of this essay, she goes on to assert that non-liturgical material was also copied during the period (1989: 170).

Byrne's introduction to O'Neill's *The Irish Hand* examines the art of writing from that period and concludes that 'a series of legends and traditions ... all suggest, what seems to be confirmed by the language of our earliest texts, that it was in the 630s that vernacular lore, legal, genealogical and literary, was first committed to writing' (1984:xvi). This would confirm Stevenson's view that the advent of literacy in Irish can be dated as early as the first half of the sixth century, since there is generally a gap between literacy and literature of about a century, or even longer.

The script employed by the scribes, that most essential literary tool, was clearly borrowed from the Latin but went beyond it and seems to have been 'a deliberate creation out of elements of the several scripts inherited from antiquity which the earliest missionaries had brought with them' (Bieler 1966: 17). If so, this implies a knowledge of those scripts and, more critically, a profound understanding of their functionality, neither of which would have been possible without a highly developed literacy throughout the learned class.

A tribute to the ingenuity of that class in devising *de novo* a script for the language is that, according to Bieler 'of all the numerous types of Latin script which came into existence during the early Middle Ages, the Irish script has had the longest life and the widest dissemination' (1966: 15). In short, the script was perfectly adapted to the needs of the language it served and expertly equipped for the task of writing. As such, it was a major achievement in what would now be termed the development of software, and an aesthetically attractive one at that.

On the basis of the above analyses, it is reasonable to conclude that what we refer to as the beginnings of Irish writing took place in a sophisticated, literate society which had moulded the technique of writing to its own distinct purposes and applied it not only to the language from which it had imported that technique, but also to its own language, the Irish of the day. Few contemporary cultures could make the same claim.

Use of the vernacular

This achievement of putting pen on parchment in the Irish vernacular has been attributed by many scholars to a number of sociological factors born out of the country's geography, history and its culture of learning. These combined to create what Stevenson calls 'a unique situation' which, in turn, explains 'the astonishing cultural confidence one sees in the sixth and seventh centuries' (1989: 165). By this she means that the *filid* of early medieval Ireland mastered the craft of literacy rather than allowing it to master them: 'Christianity, with all the new learning and international perspectives it brought with it, did not supersede the native culture, but had to come to terms with it' (1989: 165).

One intriguing example of this accommodation is Carney's contention that what made Ireland different from other parts of contemporary Europe 'was that the vernacular was used as a medium of instruction. The student had to learn to read it, to write it' (1969: 164). This seems clear enough from many of the glosses, among the earliest examples of Old Irish writing (taken here in the two senses of that word), for they are by nature either the sort of notes that any well organised lecturer would prepare for class, or else the type of jottings that any prudent student would write down for later use (Dillon 1954a: 10).

Although Carney placed us in his debt with his insight, he does not explain why Irish should have been the medium of instruction, a far more interesting and significant sociological question. He does, however, use it as a credible explanation for the production of some genres of the literature when he goes on to argue that 'no literary language can be taught without adequate reading matter' (1969: 164), which is true enough.

But this is merely a partial explanation since it does not account for the production of other genres, such as law, poetry and sacred material, the existence of which is proof positive of the dominance of the vernacular as the standard medium of communication for many, if not most, secular and sacred activities of the day. And it is this dominance that excites speculation as to why it should have occurred.

Irrespective of the cultural factors at work, which led initially to a vigorous, if unexpected, bilingualism in the centuries immediately succeeding the arrival of Christianity, it appears from the evidence that 'by the end of the ninth century Irish was fast replacing Latin as the chief means of written communication in the monastic schools, and the change is reflected in the annals' (Byrne 1984: xix).

This is the reverse, as said earlier, of what could have been anticipated and, perhaps, the real reason is that the arrival of Latin did not go hand in hand with the sort of political, social, administrative and economic convulsion that attended its appearance in what became provinces of the Roman Empire, nor, for that matter, with the cultural earthquake that followed the destruction of the Gaelic order nearly a thousand years later.

In short, the use of the vernacular is evidence of cultural continuity between pagan and Christian Ireland. The society remained more or less intact as it entered the mainstream of medieval Europe. Latin enriched, but did not supplant, the indigenous culture. In the modern idiom of sociology it can be said that the Latin culture was internalised and became part of a new vibrant integral whole, which was simultaneously national and European. The balance between the two elements was dynamic, with the weight shifting progressively towards the vernacular. Making its appearance 'as early as the seventh century'

(Stevenson, 1989: 162), it was fast replacing Latin as the main means of literary communication three centuries later, as was previously noted (Byrne 1984: xix). The literary evidence all points in this direction and seems to be consistent with the analysis offered above.

If, as Carney claims, traditions were written down 'in the earliest period of Irish literature' (1983: 127) and if some of this material can be dated 'to about 600' (125) or, perhaps, 'about 600 AD or earlier' (112) then it is timely to examine 'this substantial body of extremely early Irish, some of which is arguably dated to the fifth century' (Stevenson, 1989: 152).

The glosses

In Ó Cuiv's reckoning there are about 350 manuscripts of Irish provenance from this period, scattered, in the main, across continental Europe. But, of these, only about fifty contain glosses (Ó Cathasaigh 1996: 59).

We are thus left with the sobering reflection that, apart from the Ogam inscription, our access to contemporary sources depends, first, on the caprice of history, whereby some manuscripts escaped destruction, fortuitously in sufficient number to provide the requisite bulk of material to reconstruct the language and, second, to the vagaries of human nature which led some scribes or students, but not others, to write down their notes or marginalia on these same manuscripts. The degree of randomness in this whole process is frightening. A combination of chance circumstances, involving the preservation of some manuscripts and the personal decision of some scholars to write on what must have been precious books (a practice usually discouraged) has left us with the key to Old Irish literature. It so easily could have been otherwise.

As is well known, these glosses were assembled by Zeuss, who in the 1830s, 'conceived the plan of collecting in the libraries of the great Irish foundations abroad the relics of the early Irish language. He searched in Würzburg, in St. Gall, in Milan' (Dillon 1954a: 9) and 'began to work in earnest upon (these) earliest manuscript records of Irish' (McCone 1996a: 12). Because of historical chance playing another beneficent role, he was able to use the Latin texts to decipher their Old Irish translations, ironically reversing the original intention of the glossators. Latin was used to translate Old Irish, something that would have been impossible had not the literati of medieval Ireland been bilingual. The contribution of Zeuss went way beyond the incredible labour of transcribing thousands of glosses, since he then used them to compile his famous *Grammatica Celtica* in 1853 (Dillon 1954a: 9). This in turn allowed subsequent scholars, such as Thurneysen, to develop a deeper understanding of the grammar and to begin the task of translating material which, up to then, had been beyond the capacity of even O'Donovan and O'Curry (Dillon 1954a: 9).

The seminal importance of the glosses is attested by Thurneysen himself in his introduction to *A Grammar of Old Irish*. He notes that for the grammarian the most important sources of Old Irish are those preserved in more or less contemporary manuscripts (1946: 4), the viewpoint to which all scientific scholarship subscribes. And he confirms that the most important of these are in Würzburg and Milan, adding, Turin, Karlsruhe, Leyden, St. Gall, St. Paul in Corinthia, Vienna and Berlin, as well as *The Book of Armagh*. 'Much of this material was edited and translated by Whitley Stokes and John Strachan in the *Thesaurus Palaeohibernicus*' (Ó Cathasaigh 1996: 59), with the following aim: 'to facilitate the study of the interesting and difficult language commonly called Old Irish, and for this purpose to put scholars in possession of trustworthy materials in a convenient and comparatively cheap combination' (Stokes and Strachan 1901: xi).

In this they did indeed succeed. Within the 1200 pages of this magnificent scholarly compilation can be found virtually all of the known examples of contemporaneous writing in Old Irish. This assemblage of fragments is the stuff from which Old Irish has been reconstructed. As McManus says, 'Old Irish, the language of the eighth and ninth centuries, is the earliest period sufficiently well documented to provide for a complete grammar. The manuscript records of Early Old Irish (seventh century) are just about enough to whet the appetite' (1991: 83). Most importantly, there is sufficient evidence in the glosses to permit reasonably accurate dating of material found in later manuscripts which go back to the Old Irish period.

By combining this manuscript material with the insights provided by the glosses into Old Irish grammar and vocabulary, it is possible to reconstruct something close to the Old Irish originals of much that survives only in later manuscripts. For that reason it is now appropriate to examine those manuscripts as a source for Old Irish literature.

The manuscripts

'The oldest known manuscript to have contained Old Irish saga material is the lost *Cín Dromma Snechtai* written in the first half of the eighth century' (Byrne 1984: xvi). The *Book of Armagh*, one of the ten manuscripts from before the year 1000 which have survived on Irish soil (Kenney 1929: 7) is, in fact, 'the oldest manuscript to contain examples of connected Irish prose narrative, as distinct from the disjointed glosses and sentences found in earlier Latin manuscripts' (Byrne 1984: xv). Written in 807 or 808 (Stokes and Strachan 1901: xiv), it contains a transcript of older documents. But the earliest manuscript 'to contain secular material, prose and verse, in Old and Middle Irish is the twelfth-century *Lebor na hUidre*, written, or at least completed at Clonmacnoise' (Byrne 1984: xv).

There is, therefore, a gap of about three hundred years between the *Book of Armagh* and *Lebor na hUidre*, causing McCone to emphasise that 'contemporary manuscript sources for the eleventh century are so far virtually confined to a few marginal notes and poems in manuscripts dated to the latter half of that century' (1996a: 35). Thus, the first substantial sources of material are to be found in 'the big three of the twelfth century, namely *Lebor na hUidre*, *Rawlinson B502* and the *Book of Leinster*' (*ibid.*).

This graphically illustrates the problem of dealing with the beginnings of writing in Old Irish. The earliest glosses belong to the eighth century but the earliest substantial continuous pieces of secular prose belong to the twelfth, 'a time when the vernacular was already nearer to Modern Irish than Old Irish' (Greene 1954: 26). Indeed, the problem is exacerbated by the reality that 'much ancient matter survives only in manuscripts from the fourteenth and fifteenth centuries ... so that when we say that a composition is from, say the eighth century, we mean no more than it is stylistically and linguistically compatible with that period' (1954: 26).

In other words, because 'the manuscripts are very often much more recent in date than the composition of the texts they record ... the texts will usually have been subjected to varying degrees of revision, modernization and corruption' (McManus 1991: 32).

Describing the text which he chose as the basis for his translation of the *Táin*, for example, Thomas Kinsella says it 'is the work of many hands and in places is little more than the mangled remains of miscellaneous scribal activities' (1969: xi); his description gives a flavour of what actually confronts a scholar in trying to reconstruct an Old Irish text. The manuscripts are therefore a mixed bag of sources, varying in language, completeness of material, editorial objectivity and, of course, age. More accurately they could be described as a ragbag of history's leavings, which, in a scientific sense, are in no way a representative sample of the whole. They are simply what we have, not what we would choose to have, nor what, as in the case of the *Annals of the Four Masters*, was carefully chosen for us to have.

This state of affairs mirrors the chance occurrences which determined the preservation of the glosses. They are two sides of the same historic coin, which Kenney describes as being partly due to the ravages of the Vikings, 'the torch of the sea-kings' as he poetically describes them, and due also to what he calls, with masterful understatement, 'later times of trouble' (1929: 9). The combination of these two forces have left us, as said earlier, with only ten manuscripts on Irish soil dating from before 1000, most of which are written in Latin (1929: 9). What does remain in Irish is the result of chance, like the glosses, but in this case a more vengeful and capricious chance. Dillon's account of the discovery of leaves from the *Yellow Book of Lecan* by Dr. Best, containing the complete text of *The Wooing of Étaín* (1968: 19), is but one example of how dependent we are on random historical events for access to manuscript records.

It might have been even worse had the Normans not pursued a different policy from that of the Cromwellian planters five hundred years later. Unlike what occurred in Norman England, the Anglo-Normans in Ireland did not bring about 'a complete cultural break with the past ... the ancient texts were still copied century after century so that poems of the seventh and eighth centuries have survived in unique copies written nine hundred years later ... The vast bulk of early Irish literature in prose and verse ... is to be attributed to this fact' (Byrne 1984: xxiv). So, in order to get back to the original texts, copies (of copies of copies) made five hundred years or more later have to be debugged of intervening corruption. The manuscripts, unfortunately, are no carbon copies or photostats of the originals. But, for all that, they are an authentic source from which a minute, but not necessarily representative, portion of what must have been first written in Old Irish can be retrieved and reconstructed.

Describing the manuscripts as 'miniature libraries', Dillon says that for the most part they are 'miscellaneous collections of prose and verse, sacred and profane. We find legend, history and hagiography, bardic poetry and lyric poetry, medical and legal tracts, Old, Middle and Modern Irish, side by side' (1948: xvii). Thanks to these anthologies, we can sift out Old Irish texts, apply the linguistic analysis developed on the basis of the glosses and be put in direct contact with one of Europe's oldest vernacular literatures. Just how old this literature is has already begun to emerge through the course of this essay so far, but it is necessary, nonetheless, to attempt some definitive conclusions.

Antiquity

The antiquity of writing in Irish has been the subject of vigorous debate among scholars since the discipline first emerged. But the debate can, perhaps, be fairly summarised as one concerning the antiquity of the subject matter, i.e. whether the manuscripts contain the transcriptions of a pre-existing oral tradition or are literary compositions in their own right, first written down in the scriptoria of the fifth or sixth and subsequent centuries. Important as this question may be, it does not detract from the fact that the vernacular literature dates at least from the sixth century onwards in terms of being physically committed to parchment.

If that narrower definition of the origins of early Irish literature is accepted, then what can be stated with confidence is that 'Ireland possesses the most extensive early vernacular literature in medieval Europe, going back to the sixth century at least and perhaps earlier' (Stevenson 1989: 127). Indeed, even that vigorous scourge of the 'nativist school' (of which more later), Carney, asserts that 'the bulk of early Irish literature has been assigned linguistically to the eighth or ninth centuries, and a small proportion to the seventh, even to the sixth' (1983: 113).

McCone, who has taken the baton from Carney, agrees with this dating: 'In addition to a very substantial Latin literature early Christian Ireland boasts by far the most extensive and diverse vernacular literature in medieval Europe. The period from the fifth to the twelfth century abounds in Latin, Old and Middle Irish and bilingual texts' (1990: 1).

So, irrespective of the scholarly stance on the provenance or purpose of the literature, there is virtually unanimous agreement on its antiquity. The dispute, which is so comprehensively addressed by McCone (1990), is really about the antiquity of the content: is it older than the medium in which it is first recorded? The answer constitutes an essay in itself but, for present purposes, it suffices to say that the antiquity of the literature is, per se, beyond dispute. It is the oldest of its kind in Europe.

Diversity and content

Aside from its antiquity, the other distinguishing feature of Old Irish literature is its diversity. McCone lists what he describes as 'a wide range of genres' (1990: 1), while Kenney sets out what he calls 'the chief classes of texts' (1929: 4), both of which cover more than twenty categories of literature.

Dillon reminds us, however, that the corpus contains 'no drama and no rhetoric and that, although there is plenty of historical material, there is nothing in Irish that one can set beside Herodotus or Thucydides or Livy or

Caesar until Geoffrey Keating compiled his great narrative. In Ireland, as in Wales, poetry and legend are the substance of literature' (1948: xix).

This is too narrow a definition, since it would confine literature to works of the imagination and exclude large swathes of learning generally considered to be an integral part of literature, such as biography, philosophy, science, law and theology. For the purposes of this essay, the broader definition employed by McCone and Kenney is taken as a more tenable description of the 'substance of literature'.

Nevertheless, Dillon's reference to the centrality of poetry is valuable as a reminder that the diversity of Old Irish literature can be viewed not just in terms of its content or substance, but also in terms of the literary forms employed. The variety of material in verse form in Old, and also Middle Irish, is nearly as extensive as that in prose, and the poetic form was used not just for conventional poetic purposes but as a means for treating material as diverse as law, history and religious topics (Breatnach 1996: 65). Breatnach, in fact, identifies no less than seventeen categories of Old Irish literature in which verse is employed as either the sole or main medium. The literature is, therefore, a rich mix of prose, poetry and a combination of both, ranging across most of the genres to be found in other classical literatures.

If there are notable gaps in the repertoire, as Dillon pointed out, these are compensated for by a more exciting and arresting development of some genres, such as the saga and poetry. Perhaps the saga is the literature's most distinct contribution to European culture, exemplifying, as it does, 'the tension between reality and fantasy that characterises all Celtic art' (Gantz 1981: 1) so that, while it is true that early Irish literature has no Livy or Tacitus, it is equally true that Roman literature has no *Táin*, the *Aeneid* notwithstanding.

Indeed, one foreign scholar, Nagy, says this corpus of vernacular literature 'is of remarkable diversity and heterogeneity, both antiquarian and attuned to contemporary issues' (1997: 10), as will briefly be attested below. But in an unusual approach to the nature of its content, he also adds that 'arguably no other corpus originating from the impact of Christianity upon a native tradition offers such a spectacular wealth of reflexive analysis' (1997: 7).

This assessment reintroduces that tantalising question discussed earlier: the sudden flowering of a complete and complex literature on the stony soil of illiteracy. What is to be discovered in the manuscripts is 'not the beginning of a literature', according to Watkins, 'but the full flowering of a long tradition' (McCone 1996a: 19). Leaving aside the criticisms which other elements of this passage merit from McCone and Breatnach, it puts the spotlight on one feature of the literature, particularly the sagas, which immediately captures the attention of the reader. This is no adolescent fumbling for literary forms or language; it is already a fully formed adult literature. Now it is, of course, possible that, like Furriskey in Flann O'Brien's *At-Swim-Two-Birds*, the literature was born as an early adult (and, like Furriskey, without a memory of childhood), but this seems unlikely. Even Carney, that benchmark of agnosticism, confesses that the *Táin*, 'as it exists, presents us with the boyhood deeds of Cú Chulainn in a remarkably artistic fashion' (1983: 121), and he admits that the saga as a whole is 'very sophisticated narrative', which has 'no relationship whatsoever to the humble folk tale' (1983: 115).

The remarkable artistry to which Carney was attracted can be seen in the *Táin*, not only in its characterisation and the realism with which it portrays the national politics of the day (Carney 1983: 115), but also in the centrality given to dialogue (Nagy 1997: 5), the pillow talk being the most colourful example. The opening lines could be taken for one of Neil Simon's better scenes in a Broadway hit.

The freshness, originality and force of the dialogue have all the hallmarks of an accomplished pen, with an acute understanding of the psychology of women. If Medb's reasons for choosing Aillil as a husband – and it is noteworthy that she did the choosing – can be bettered by any piece from another literature, even Sophocles, then such a piece is not as widely available or accessible as one might expect. The poetry of the period is similarly mature and confident and, despite his many grumblings about the 'fundamental brainwork' being missing (an echo of Bergin's critique), Frank O'Connor ends up saying that whatever its faults, early Irish literature 'glows by its own light, the literature of a people full of confidence in itself' (1959: xi). O'Connor goes on to describe this literature as one 'of which no Irishman need feel ashamed' (1959: xv); praise indeed from such a bored and worldly-wise savant.

To conclude with a final observation on poetry, that pinnacle of creative literature, Murphy says that 'Irish lyric poetry is unique in the Middle Ages in freshness of spirit and perfection of form', even if modelled on early continental Latin hymn-meters (1956: xiii-xiv). The poetry of Old Irish demonstrates not just a love of nature (as in 'The king and the hermit') or of God, but is shot through with Nagy's introspection about such matters as personal loss ('Liadan tells of her love for Cuirithir'), sacrifice ('King and hermit'), humour ('Ungenerous payment') or just life itself as it is lived ('The scholar and his cat'). Once again, there is a maturity of poetic sensitivity which belies the late arrival of Latin literacy and points to a culture in full flood. It is, to be sure, nothing to be ashamed of; rather it is something to be wondered at. The lyric poetry is unique, and it is testimony, along with the sagas and other genres, to the claim that the beginnings of Irish writing provide us with a literature that stands apart from its European contemporaries in terms of content, diversity and the use of imagination. As MacNeill says of its authors: 'to them the marvellous was the familiar, and their literature did not shrink from it' (1921: 16). Instead, they embraced it.

Varieties

As stated earlier, Kenney (1929: 4) and McCone (1990: 1) between them list about twenty varieties of literature produced in the Old Irish period. Without claiming any scientific basis or logic for the classification, they can be grouped under the broad headings of history (historical narrative and verse, genealogies, origin legends and annals), law (lay and religious), imaginative literature (sagas and poetry), scientific (topography, grammar and astronomy), sociology and politics (prerogatives of kings and people, customary duties), tradition (proverbial literature) and religious (biblical exegesis, liturgy, lives of saints). Neither this categorisation of genres nor the placing of particular texts under each heading is exhaustive, but such an exercise is illustrative of the enormous output of the period and indicative of a raw cultural energy that quickly mastered so many forms and types of literature.

Because the Irish were, and still are, 'extremely interested in their history, more so, it would seem, than their contemporaries' (Byrne 1965: 38), it is a good place to start. Whatever about the reasons for this interest, the Irish seemed to prefer their history 'in the form of historical fiction' (*ibid.*). Intent for reasons of racial pride, it would seem, on equipping themselves with a historical pedigree no less noble nor ancient than the other great civilisations of the time, they invented a pseudo-history stretching back to the Flood itself.

The *Lebor Gabála*, or *Book of Invasions*, is the best known of these inventions. It is typical of what Nagy calls 'etiological narratives in which literature is figured as a means of preserving what society needs to know from and about its past' (1997: 7), and it would seem that the process began soon after the advent of literacy since 'perhaps as early as the seventh century, the Irish monastic network was being employed in the manufacture of tribal origin legends, and, in the process, in the dissemination of secular saga' (Byrne 1984: xviii).

This obsession with history accounts for the preoccupation in early Irish literature with genealogies and the origin legends mentioned by Byrne. These genres immediately stand out as a defining characteristic of the historical literature produced, a feature that lasted in the literature to the seventeenth century and beyond. It accounts too for the annals, which began to be compiled as early as the seventh century.

It can be accepted, on the one hand, that these texts enshrine the traditions and history of the country, but, on the other, one has to be conscious that they were distorted by the annalists and scribes, particularly for the early centuries (Martin 1975: 7). The earliest of the annals may well be 'an Ulster Chronicle', which MacNeill believed to have been compiled in 712 and O'Rahilly in 740 (Mac Niocaill 1975: 19). There seems to be evidence of an even earlier 'series of annalistic notes compiled at Bangor in the course of the sixth and seventh centuries' (Byrne 1984: xvi), although Mac Niocaill describes the evidence for Bangor as 'shaky' (1975: 19). Other known early sources are the *Book of Cuana*, with linguistic forms later than the early-ninth century, and the *Book of Dub dá Leithe* (1975: 20).

Notwithstanding the fact that they are a mixture of historical fact and fiction, the very existence of the annals is a literary fact. They are part of the corpus of material produced in the beginning of Irish literature, and they served later scholars as an invaluable repository of early Irish history, which the Four Masters did so much to preserve and Keating to popularise at the very moment the Gaelic order was in its death throes.

As Dr. Johnson once observed, the Irish are a very litigious people and it is hardly any wonder that law played a central role in early Irish society, or that it should have been amongst the first elements of learning to be committed to writing. The sheer scale of the enterprise can be gauged from the fact that Binchy's *Corpus Iuris Hibernici*, published in 1978, provides 'a reasonably complete diplomatic edition of the Old Irish and later legal material, amounting to over 2300 pages' (Breatnach 1996a: 109). It is the sheer volume of material here that impresses, whatever its origins – again a subject of vigorous debate among scholars.

It is very likely that the main impetus behind the committal to writing came from the Church, even though the laws are often in conflict with canon law (Byrne 1984: xviii). Indeed, legal manuscripts use the same spelling system, script, punctuation, abbreviations and illuminated capitals as are found in manuscripts of monastic origin (Kelly 1988: 232). But, as ever, there is disagreement about the authors: were they professional lay jurists or clerics, or both?

The debate is well summarised by Kelly (1988: 232–38), and suffice it to say that the evidence points in the direction of clerical authorship. He notes, for example, that Ó Corráin, Breatnach and Breen have drawn attention 'to the extent to which Old Irish law-texts are based on canon law', and that Ó Corráin has concluded the law tracts 'are the work of a single class of learned men' (1988: 233).

As with much of the other material from the Old Irish period, 'the manuscripts in which the law texts are found date mainly from the fourteenth to the sixteenth centuries, but the linguistic evidence shows many of these texts were originally written in the seventh to eighth centuries' (1988: 225). The authors are obviously well informed about the topics with which they are dealing and, in addition to their technical knowledge, show great ingenuity in their treatment of legal problems, sometimes over-ingenuity. In general, they are a sound guide to early Irish legal institutions (1988: 237-38).

The most important of the Old Irish compilations is that known as the *Senchas Már*, the great [collection of] traditional law texts. These texts range in date from the seventh to the eighth centuries, and were probably brought together before the middle of the eighth century (1988: 245). Even though the secular law tracts set down what can be termed civil law, Ó Corráin and Breatnach 'have pointed to a pervasive scriptural, patristic and canonistic influence upon them and made an incontrovertible case for monastic authorship' (McCone 1990: ix).

Consequently, McCone believes that all early Irish law 'betrays the Old Testament stamp so typical of the early medieval Irish learned classes' overall outlook' (1990: 102), which contrasts with what Breatnach describes as 'the naive acceptance of the traditional account of the genesis of Irish law' (1996a: 114).

Leaving aside this question of Church influence on the authors of the law tracts, the approach to legal problems in the texts themselves is fair and humane, within the limits set by the strictly hierarchical structure of the society (Kelly 1988: 236). In this regard, the law tracts tell us a great deal about the society of the day and reveal one that was not just humane, or even advanced on matters such as divorce, but deeply learned and reflective in an area of social organisation, which only a highly developed civilisation can master.

The scientific, religious, sociological and political material of the period is too diverse and copious to permit succinct encapsulation, but, here again, it is indicative of a high state of learning, at least in terms of its own times. In passing, it can also be said that the law texts demonstrate the capacity of the Old Irish language to handle any issue, however complex or technical, in an expert fashion; another example of that tantalising question as to how literacy could have been matched so fruitfully with learning in such a short period of time. The same comment has already been made of the imaginative literature, mainly saga and poetry, which could only have been produced, according to MacNeill writing specifically of the *Táin*, 'in a period of great exaltation' (1921: 16).

Conclusion

Perhaps that insight regarding 'great exaltation' provides the psychological explanation for the rich outpourings of early Irish writings. That this exaltation was produced by a marriage of the native and Latin cultures is something on which virtually all scholars seem united, irrespective of other differences between them. Nobody, it seems, would contest Dillon's claim that the early adaptation of the vernacular tradition by the monks 'is one of the remarkable facts of Irish history' (1954a: 7).

Put another way, it was the use of the vernacular to record it that made Irish history so remarkable. Carney's 'miracle' is to be found, for all who want to travel the road to a new Rome, in the beginnings of Old Irish writing. It is a journey of great trouble, no doubt, but also one of great reward.

Chapter 2

Hierarchical, Egalitation, Aristocratic:

status in early Irish Society

Summary

This essay analyses status in early Irish society from the perspective of political science. The society is first considered in terms of the structure common to the broad Indo-European culture. The basic features marking out early Ireland as sui generis are next identified, with the focus on its hierarchical and aristocratic nature, which was openly based on the concept of inequality.

The complex system of social stratification is then analysed on the basis of the main law tracts, with particular attention devoted to the distinction drawn between privileged and non-privileged freemen. The seven grades of the privileged aristocracy, who are the sole landowners, are detailed by rank and function, with particular reference to honour-price and clientship as the most unique features of the system. The various grades of non-noble freemen are briefly discussed, and a résumé of the unfree status by rank is presented.

The essay concludes that the concept of status provided social stability in early Irish society, and that the potential for mobility between ranks allowed for internal renewal of society. Viewed in the round, they system around which early Irish society was organised emerges as one which was extraordinarily sophisticated.

Introduction

Status in any society is determined by a number of factors. Wealth, birth and profession may be regarded as the three basic determinants. But a more fundamental consideration is the philosophy pertaining to the nature of man.

Feudal societies were based on the principle that men were unequal simply by reason of birth, a feature that can more easily be seen in societies structured on a rigid caste system. In these social systems, status was conferred at birth and lasted permanently throughout life. Under the impulse of the Reformation and the industrial revolution, the broad European culture developed the concept that the individual could determine his or her place in society by virtue of personal effort, thus allowing for an element of mobility between ranks or castes.

Beginning with the American and French revolutions, modern democratic societies have advanced further to the single premise that all men and women are equal, simply by being men or women. Consequently, status in society is an accident of circumstance, and not a preordained privilege granted by fate. At the root of any democratic society is the egalitarian concept that people are equal in the political and legal sense, even if there is economic and social inequality as a consequence of market forces.

Indo-European cultures, which precede feudal societies, differ substantially from these better known models in respect of status and display a variety of common characteristics relating to social organisation. The overriding political necessity of these cultures, an in-depth analysis of which lies outside the scope of this essay, was that society should be so structured that certain essential functions were discharged in a predictable and permanent manner, thus ensuring external security and internal stability. It could be said that status was a function of these primary social objectives. Furthermore, it could be argued that, as a direct consequence, a philosophy emerged which was firmly rooted in the precept that people were inherently unequal.

This is clearly obvious from the caste system in Indian society, with which early Irish society shared a number of striking similarities (Dillon, 1947). It is also seen in the Roman Republic with its division into patricians, equites and plebs, and slaves as is often forgotten.

Early Irish society belongs to this family of cultures, and that particular historical context serves as a backdrop for the following analysis. It will be seen that it had certain social characteristics which made it *sui generis*, but which can be readily understood in the larger Indo-European context to which early Irish society properly belongs.

Basic features of early Irish society

Various authors have defined early Irish society as hierarchical, aristocratic and inegalitarian. Ó Corráin describes it as intensely aristocratic (1972: 42), Binchy as instinctively hierarchical (1954: 56) and Kelly as both hierarchical and inegalitarian (1988: 7).

If law is to be taken as the handmaiden of politics (a viewpoint with which lawyers might take issue), then it follows naturally that the Roman principle of equality before the law did not apply in early Irish society. That principle is defined by Binchy as meaning that every adult who was both free and *sui iuris* enjoyed equal status and capacity (1941: xviii).

Kelly reaffirms this analysis by commenting that native Irish law never subscribed to the Roman principle of 'all citizens being equal before the law' (1988: 7), although he immediately adds that early Irish lawyers were familiar with the principle from canon law, quoting both *Bretha Crólige* and the '*Introduction to the Senchas Már*' in evidence (8). Nevertheless, as MacNeill observes, one of the most obvious characteristics of ancient Irish law is that it is the law of a limited and privileged class (1923: 266).

This apparent disjunction between secular and canon law merely reflected the compelling need for the legal system to buttress a functioning social structure. As an integral part of a sophisticated and complex culture it could not be plucked out of its natural setting and refashioned for purposes which were foreign to the nature of the society and which remained faithful to the Indo-European model. In that regard, the all-pervasive feature of early Irish society was the relationship between the community and the land, or differently expressed, between the people and nature.

The sacral role of the king, as personifying the people, has been well established by scholars, as has the supporting sacred roles of other office holders, dignitaries or professions. Essentially, the king married nature so that it became an ally by marriage, hence the inauguration rite whereby a new king 'slept' with the earth goddess, and his fidelity to that marriage was blessed with the fruits of nature in phraseology which is a conventional feature of the sagas, praise poetry and wisdom texts. In an agricultural economy, with only the rudiments of scientific knowledge at its disposal, this was a common-sense communal response to the destructive potential of nature in terms of weather, climate and plague.

Again, it follows as a matter of course that the fundamental distinction between people is that some are sacred, *nemed* being the term with the basic (but not exclusive) meaning of 'sacred, holy' (Kelly 1988: 9), while the rest are non-*nemed*, i.e. non-sacred and non-holy. In the *Uraiceacht Becc* the category termed *nemed* comprises all persons of free status and this association of free status with 'holiness' dates from the time when freemen were 'holy', or privileged, in the sense of being qualified to participate in public religious rites (MacNeill 1923: 266).

Later, as society evolved, people are also divided into free and unfree, *sóer* and *dóer*, for social and economic reasons. On top of this, it is inevitable in a society with a developed sense of the role which each individual must perform for the common good that these divisions into the sacred and non-sacred, the free and the unfree, should each be ranked in accordance with their religious, political and social and economic significance.

Complex classification

When all these variables are taken into account, early Irish society emerges as one that is highly structured into a complex classification by status and rank. Consequently, as MacNeill observes, the most distinctive feature of ancient Irish law is the law of status and, to the minds of the Irish jurists, this law was the most important part of their jurisprudence (1923: 265).

Yet, two features of the system give it a coherence consistent with the underlying philosophy and economic realities on which the society is based. Each individual who is free has a clearly defined legal status and capacity. And every such individual is given an honour-price consistent with, or deriving from, his or her position in the hierarchy (Kelly 1988: 11). Honour-price is defined by MacNeill as the valuation of the freeman's status, not a valuation for a life or for a year, but a valuation of the power and effect of the person's status at any given time (1923: 270). Moreover, in conformity with economic and social realities, that honour-price is determined in terms of units of currency expressed in cattle or female slaves.

There are, of course, other dimensions to what might seem a rigid stratification of society for ideological, theological or religious reasons. It is inevitable that birth and property should actually play a role in the determination or assignation of rank in any society. As the concept of kinship confirms, birth played a pre-eminent part in conferring status on an individual, for reasons of social stability; hence, the justification for Ó Corráin's claim that the society was intensely aristocratic.

But one does not need to be a Marxist to recognise instinctively that in any society property also confers status, indeed it is frequently a *sine qua non* of rank. Membership of the Roman patrician class, for example, depended on the value of property holdings in land and, until the advent of universal suffrage as late as the last century, property determined the right of franchise in so-called democracies.

Social mobility

Consequently, social function, birth and wealth are inextricably interwoven in the actual determination of status. But early Irish society was sufficiently intelligent to recognise that these demarcations should not be so rigid that they became an obstacle to economic progress, or worse, a threat to communal survival. Consequently, a distinguishing feature of the early Irish social system was the potential for mobility between ranks, unlike in the caste system of India.

Movement in either direction was possible in early Irish society for two reasons: the loss or the acquisition of the necessary qualifications. A *nemed* could be degraded into a 'small person' for conduct unbecoming of rank or the failure to sustain the appropriate property qualification (as measured in clients, which was a surrogate for property holdings or wealth). Likewise, mobility in the opposite direction was possible, perhaps encouraged, by elevation into the ranks of the *nemed* because of increased wealth or an individual's art or God-given talent (Kelly 1988: 12).

The author of the text on status, the *Uraiceacht Becc*, offers the legal maxim *ferr fer a chiniud* ('a man is better than his birth'). This is an extraordinarily intelligent insight into the social and economic dynamic that any society requires if it is to survive by continuous internal renewal and, if proven to have been applied extensively, would favourably distinguish early Irish society from the Indian, or even the Roman, model.

Status and Rank

According to Kelly (1988: 9), three law texts mainly dealing with rank in early Irish society have survived: *Críth Gablach*, *Uraiceacht Becc* and *Míad*slechta*. They differ among themselves in some respects and, as Kelly puts it, 'their detailed classifications of rank can only have borne a limited resemblance to reality'.

Binchy goes further with this latter point when he states in his introduction to *Críth Gablach* that it is impossible to believe 'they were ever applied so rigidly and meticulously as they appear' in the text (1941: xix). He adds that the text is characterised by 'an extreme, and at times ludicrous, schematism', which should only be regarded as a theoretical construction bearing only a very limited relation to the realities of life in ancient Ireland.

Neither scholar, however, expands on his belief that the texts are ideal rather than actual representations of society as it existed.

MacNeill, on the other hand, takes a more rounded and pragmatic view of the law tracts. He argues that despite its artificial appearance, the system of classification by grades was an actual and important factor in the everyday practical working of the laws. The only way a person's honour-price could be determined was by assigning him or her to a particular grade to which a particular honour-price had already been assigned (1923: 266).

Hence, the classification was no mere matter of juristic theory, but a social necessity. This judgement by MacNeill, coming as it does from a man who was a politician as well as a scholar, can be taken as a closer approximation to the truth than those of the other two authorities cited above. Consequently, the following schema, taken from the Uraicecht Becc, can be regarded as a working model of status in early Irish society.

Using the sacred/non-sacred and free/unfree divisions referred to earlier, the first thing to be said is that people are essentially divided into four broad classes, from the king down to the slave. Each class is characterised by reference to the status of an individual as follows:

- *nemed*
- non-*nemed* freeman
- *dóer*, or *unfree*
- slaves

Each of these social classes is internally divided on the basis of rank, which in turn, is determined by the social variables discussed at the outset. But, since the primary determinant of status is *nemed* or non-*nemed*, this matter is now discussed, and is followed by an analysis of honour-price, which is the primary determinant of rank.

Nemed

The noble *nemed* class was composed of the aristocracy and noble professions, obviously including church dignitaries following the arrival of Christianity.

They are privileged in that they are free, take precedence socially and politically and land is in their exclusive possession. While no *nemed* is entirely above the law, the members of this class also enjoy certain legal privileges and are immune from a number of legal obligations. For example, procedures for the distraint of their property are different from procedures applying to other free persons and are difficult to enforce; this is a reasonable provision, since wealth is a condition for continued membership of the class, and hence ownership must be safeguarded to the greatest extent possible, especially against vexatious actions. Some law tracts emphasise that a contract with a *nemed* is unenforceable, presumably for the same social reason.

In legal terms, the property requirement for membership of the nobility was expressed in the possession of clients, this being a surrogate for wealth, as will be seen later. Each grade of *nemed*, accordingly, carries a stipulation as to the required number of both free and base clients. Each is also described in the texts by the use of the word *aire*, with a description of function or rank attached as the distinguishing marker.

The meaning of aire is debated by Binchy in his 'Legal glossary' in *Críth Gablach* (1941: 69–109), where he states it is used to describe any freeman who possesses an independent legal status with an honour-price accruing to him by virtue of his own status (69). Occasionally, it is used in the more restricted sense of 'noble', which seems to be the case in the following classification of the *nemed* by rank.

According to some of the texts, the *nemed* were themselves divided into two broad groupings, noble and base, i.e., those who belonged to the aristocracy and learned caste and those engaged in non-agricultural professions and crafts. The latter were known as base-*nemed* to distinguish them from the nobility, and it is clear, according to Kelly (1988: 10) that they did not enjoy full *nemed* privileges. They might more accurately be described as non-noble freeman, or citizens, to borrow both a Roman and modern concept.

Dillon and Chadwick believe (1967: 97) that the old Celtic, and apparently the Indo-European, pattern of society was based on a tripartite division of warrior (*rí*), priest (*fili*) and husbandman (*aire*). MacNeill concludes that by the time the laws came to be written, about the middle of the seventh century, the original three grades of nobles had been expanded to seven in number. He states that *Críth Gablach* may well be historically correct in saying that the existence of seven orders in the clergy gave rise to a corresponding sevenfold classification of civil grades (1923: 268).

It seems clear that the social system had been in a state of evolution by the time the law tracts were committed to writing and, indeed, that they continued to evolve in the following centuries.

Hence, the two main texts, the *Uraicecht Becc* and *Críth Gablach*, do not always correspond in respect of the classification of the nobility. Leaving aside for the moment the question of the *filid* and clerics, both of which rank equal in status to the nobles, the ruling nobility are divided into seven grades, exclusive of the *bóaire* class (MacNeill 1923: 269).

This division MacNeill asserts, became the traditional doctrine of the law schools. The terms *grád *flatha*, 'noble grades', and *grád sechtae*, 'sevenfold order', were applied interchangeably to the collectivity of ruling nobles and were taken as synonymous.

The collective *grád féne*, 'order of the *Féni*', was the designation of all others of free status. These were considered as base-*nemed*, mentioned above, to distinguish them from the nobility.

Honour-price

It was suggested at the outset that the social structure of early Ireland was *sui generis*. By way of corroboration it was stated that this is borne out by the law tracts, which reveal a legal system with unique features in respect of the law of persons. In contrast to the Roman and canon law principle that all citizens or freeman are equal before the law, the point was made that the basic principle underlying early Irish law is avowedly the opposite.

Consequently, it was noted that the foundation on which the law of early irish society rests is that individuals are unequal and that each person belongs to a particular grouping in society with different rights and privileges. Hence, individual rights and legal capacity are determined by, and limited to, those pertaining to the class and rank to which each individual belongs.

On this basis it can be said that the key distinguishing characteristic of each class and rank is an honour-price, or *lóg n-enech*, which literally means 'the price of his face' (Kelly 1988: 8). And it is this unique legal device which makes the early Irish social system *sui generis*. Honour-price is the measure of a person's status in society. It determines an individual's capacity to perform most legal acts, such as entering into a contract. And it determines the compensation to be paid for any major offence committed against the person.

Most of the provisions of the law are such that, according to MacNeill, the element of honour-price entered into almost every operation of law (1923: 266). For example, an individual could not make a contract greater than his honour-price, nor could that individual go surety beyond this amount (Kelly 1988: 9). The honour-price determined a freeman's capacity to give evidence (1988: 203) and to swear a compugatory oath (201). Most particularly, it pervaded the law on personal injury, such as murder, serious injury, theft and satire.

In short, honour-price determined social status and legal capacity in early Irish society. It was the all-embracing expression of an individual's place in society. The law made no bones about the fundamental inequality inherent in the social system. It faced the issue head on. The author of *Bretha Crólige* observes that everybody has an equal honour-price in canon law, but baldly states that in native law their honour-price is unequal (Kelly 1988: 8). The *'Introduction to the Senchas Már'* goes so far as to claim that the world had equality until the distinction it introduced between king and commoner, free and unfree, rich and poor (*ibid.*).

The measure of these inequalities was the difference in honour-price attaching to each rank in society; and, hence, to every person by virtue of their status. As Kelly states so succinctly (1988: 11), the honour-price of an adult freeman derives from his rank.

Moreover, the honour-price of any dependant is a proportion of his own price, a device which ensured that all members of the family were embraced in the social classification and automatically assigned a rank and legal capacity.

Clientship

The second distinguishing feature of status, and accordingly of the early Irish legal system, is clientship. This phenomenon was, of course, part of Roman society, particularly in the period of the Republic before the civil wars. But in Ireland it took on a more pronounced significance, in that the rights and duties of a lord (*flaith*) mainly related to clients (*céili* and *aithig*). In fact, it was the possession of clients which made him a lord (Kelly 1988: 27).

As can be seen immediately, the possession of clients was simply the physical and highly visible manifestation of wealth and a living proof that a lord met the property conditions pertaining to his status. This arose because clientship was created by a lord advancing a fief of stock or land to an individual in return for food-rent, winter-hospitality and other services (*ibid.*). Applying the philosophical maxim of *nemo dat quod non habet*, the granting of the requisite number of fiefs was a tangible demonstration of wealth.

Hence, clientship served a number of purposes simultaneously. Economically, it provided the lord with an income, which if properly managed, sustained his household and increased his capital worth. Socially, it enabled him to enjoy the privileges of rank.

Politically, it enabled him to discharge his responsibilities to the king and *túath* by having manpower at his disposal, such as for civil, military or ceremonial purposes. And, finally, the continued maintenance of a client base verified his conformity with the qualifications of his rank. Viewed in the round, the system was multi-functional, and a highly sophisticated social instrument for meeting the communal needs of internal stability and external security referred to in the opening paragraphs.

It also, perforce, introduced and sustained a basic differentiation in status, in that some were served while others did the serving. As the *Uraicecht Becc* puts it, there are two kinds of *nemed* on the earth, the free and the subject. The reason why the people of every art or craft are called subject *nemed* is because they serve the free *nemed* (MacNeill 1923: 273).

But the operation of the system of clientship had another set of consequences for the determination of status and legal capacity in early Irish society. The second party to the contract was the client.

As will be seen later, clients were freeman, who did not own land but who did possess property in the form of cattle and other moveable goods. Hence, the economic relationship between the lord and client was that between a landowner and a tenant. But the legal relationship could differ in one key feature; the tenant could either retain or forego his honour-price, i.e. his status as a freeman.

Consequently, the nature of the clientship contract indirectly affected status and directly determined rank. The law texts distinguish between two types of client as a consequence of what was involved in the contract. A lord could either advance a fief to a client, or advance both a fief and a payment for the client's honour-price. In the first instance the client remained free by retaining his honour-price and was logically designated a free client or *sóerchéile*.

In the second case, the client forfeited his freedom by demising it on his lord in return for a consideration (to use modern legal terminology). Logically, a client who voluntarily assigned his honour-price to a lord was known as 'a client of submission' or *céile gíallnae*. The glosses and commentaries push the logic further by calling him a *dóerchéile*, or unfree client (Kelly 1988: 29). The consequence of these different contractual obligations is that the non-noble class of freeman was divided by status, those who remained free and those who temporarily had volunteered to be unfree.

The clientship system was hence inherently more complex than it appears at first sight. But it never obscures the fact that it rests on one class owning land, and that this class is the noble *nemed*. The nobles remain at the apex of the social system. They are ranked, in accordance with wealth, essentially expressed in clients but, equally important, in terms of the social function they are expected to perform. This prompts the question of how the noble *nemed* were categorized on the basis of rank expressed in terms of functionality.

Sevenfold division of noble *Nemed*

The sevenfold division of the nobility according to the *Uraicecht Becc* (MacNeill 1923: 274) is in the following ascending order of importance, status and, hence, of honour-price.

The term aire, employed in respect of the first five grades, is here taken to mean 'nobleman' or 'aristocrat'. The seven grades are:

- *aire déso*
- *aire échto*
- *aire tuíseo*
- *aire ard*
- *aire forgill*
- *rí túaithe*
- *rí ruirech*

In *Críth Gablach*, the seven grades are set out in two different schemas, but the following would seem to be the more authoritative (MacNeill 1923: 282; Binchy 1941: 1):

- *aire déso*
- *aire échto*
- *aire ard*

- *aire tuíseo*
- *aire forgill*
- *tánaise ríg*
- *rí*

In respect of non-royal nobility, the texts most obviously differ in assigning precedence to the aire tuíseo and aire ard. Furthermore, *Críth Gablach* introduces a grade occupied by the chosen successor to the king and so maintains the seven fold division by excluding higher kings. Nevertheless, it does recognise three categories of kings, as is seen later. Despite the difference in classification, the two schemas are substantially the same, and that of the *Uraicecht Becc* will serve as the basis of the following commentary.

Both the main texts agree that at the bottom of the hierarchy is the aire déso, possessing the minimum property required for membership of the nobility at five free and five base clients. This typical lord, as Kelly calls him (1988: 27), has a retinue (*dám*) of six persons and an honour-price of ten sets, and his title means 'nobleman or aristocrat with clients' or 'lord of vassalry' (*déso* being the genitive singular of *déis* 'vassal, vassalry'). MacNeill indicates that the term must have originated as a generic name for the whole class of ruling nobles (1923: 269).

In the *Uraicecht Becc*, the next grade of lord is given as aire échto 'lord of violent deed', whose function it is to avenge the outrages inflicted on members of the túath by those of another *túath*, according to Binchy's glossary (1941: 70-72). Binchy comments, however, that the nature of this function is not clear and is open to a number of interpretations. He believes that it is likely the *aire échto* is by birth and status a commoner of the *'bóaire* class' who is ennobled for performing a public role associated with retribution, and hence, violence.

Joyce, however, offers an interesting insight by claiming that the post was similar to that of the 'Avenger of blood' of the Jews and other ancient nations, and that part of the duties was the defence of the border of a túath (1913: 92). As he also appeared to be at the immediate service of the king, the *aire échto* could be regarded as analogous to a Minister for Defence or Head of the Armed Forces, a conclusion which seems reasonable in terms of collective political responsibility for the welfare of society based on function.

The next grade as stated is the *aire tuíseo*, literally 'lord of leadership' or 'precedence'. Binchy describes the role as that of representing kin in dealings with the king and with members of another túath. This would imply a political role at this grade, which is analogous to a combination of senator and ambassador. As such, it certainly has the ring of truth about it. While *Críth Gablach* assigns a higher ranking to this grade of lord, it seems the *Uraicecht Becc* is more logical placing the aire tuíseo above the *aire échto*, but below the grade following.

The explanation for the name of the next highest rank, aire ard, is not given in the texts in terms of function, and none is offered by MacNeill, Binchy or Kelly. But the absence of a functional title and the unique use of one immediately relating to position (*ard* = 'high') suggest this lord occupied a position of high rank in the hierarchy, with a political role analogous to a king's counsellor. This is a conventional function in any aristocratic society and is of particular political significance when important decisions of state are to be made, especially so if the state leadership is collegial rather than authoritarian. Such a lord would be tantamount to a member of the inner circle, or Privy Council in medieval England, or what would nowadays be called a government.

The highest of the non-royal grades is that of aire forgill, 'lord of superior testimony'. More to the point, the meaning of the title seems to be 'conclusive testimony' and, according to Binchy's glossary, derives from the fact that the testimony of a lord belonging to this rank outweighs that of his inferiors in all cases where there is a conflict of evidence (1941: 72). But, the title possibly refers to a public function in which the aire forgill also acted as part of a court of final appeal.

This is not too fanciful a speculation, since Kelly provides a translation of the *Airecht* text on court procedure (1988: 355) which names the five categories of court in Irish law and sets out their respective functions. It is clear that the first court, named, 'the back court', has a role analogous to a court of final appeal and its composition includes, along with the king and bishop, 'an expert in every legal language with the rank of master' (*ibid.*). This could well be the *aire forgill,* or law lord, and, at first sight, would be consistent with the system of ranking in accordance with function.

Kelly (1988: 28) lists the honour-price attaching to each grade of noble ranked in *Críth Gablach* as follows:

- *aire déso:* 10 séts
- *aire ard:* 15 séts
- *aire tuíseo:* 20 séts
- *aire forgill:* 30 séts

These lords have 10, 20, 27 and 40 clients, respectively. [Note that as units of value a cumal = 3 milch cows and a *sét* = half of a milch cow.]

In keeping with the nature of the society, the most important *nemed* in a *túath*, or statelet, is the king, known as *rí túaithe* 'king of a túath'. If such a king acquires dominance over other túatha he is generally described as a *rí túath* 'king of túatha' or *ruiri* 'great king'. In *Críth Gablach*, however, he is called the *rí buiden* 'king of bands', which Kelly notes is a term not found elsewhere (1988: 17). The highest grade of king is the provincial king *rí cóicid*, or sometimes called *rí ruirech*, 'king of great kings'.

Kelly notes that the law tracts, generally speaking, do not provide for the post of *rí Érenn* 'king of Ireland' (18). The status of each grade of kingship is reflected in, or determined by, the honour-price (Kelly 1988: 17):

- *rí túaithe:* 7 *cumals*
- *rí túath:* 8 *cumals*
- *rí cóicid:* 14 *cumals*

Division of non-*Nemed* freemen

As remarked earlier, a striking phenomenon of the early Irish social system was the mobility between ranks, subject to the law, of course.

Hence a commoner could be elevated to the ranks of the nobility in accordance with clearly defined procedures involving an intermediate grade, which might properly be described as a period of probation, since it is generally assumed that it took three generations to become a full lord (Kelly 1988: 28).

The property requirement for the transition from the highest grade of commoner, *bóaire*, to the lowest grade of lord, *aire déso*, is double that applying to the bóaire according to Críth Gablach. This is a sensible provision, as it ensures the ennobled commoner not only has the requisite property to sustain clients but also that the family concerned has demonstrated its economic capacity to sustain its wealth across the generations.

A commoner launched on this path is called a *flaith aithig* 'commoner lord' in the *Cáin Sóerraith*, and in other texts is styled *aire eter da airig;* 'an *aire* between two classes of *aire*', the first being a social, and the second a legal, description.

As stated earlier, the fundamental distinction between freemen, the aire class, is the ownership of land. All of the nobility described above are noble freemen who, crucially, are landowners. But there were also freemen who were without land yet, nevertheless, possessed property consisting of cattle and other moveable goods. To put this wealth to productive use, these freemen had, of necessity, to lease land from the landowning class on a rent paying basis, thereby establishing the relationship of lord and client described above.

Kelly observes (1988: 10) that the non-*nemed* freemen probably comprised the majority of the adult male population at the time of the law tracts. Statistically, this can easily be proven, but falls outside the scope of this essay. Two main categories of non-*nemed* were distinguished along lines roughly equivalent to large and small farmers in twentieth-century Ireland. These were the *bóaire*, with an honour-price of 5 *séts*, and the ócaire with an honour-price of 3 *séts*. Both ranks could take independent legal action and play a part in decisions affecting the túath, the two fundamental characteristics of a freeman.

According to Binchy's glossary (1941: 77), the *bóaire* class of freeholder is divided into five grades, the *aire coisring*, the *fer fothlai, aitheach ara-threba a deich, bóaire febsa* and the *mruig*fer*. He doubts whether these divisions have any basis in reality. MacNeill says that clients were all of this class (1923: 267) but does not divide them by rank. On the other hand, Joyce claims there were several ranks according to the amount of property held (1913: 158).There seems to be general agreement, however, that the highest rank is the *aire coisring* who, according to Binchy is accorded a special status by his function as head of his kin, whom he represents in their dealings with external authorities (1941: 70); hence, the meaning of the title, 'binding chief'.

The function to be performed is that of ensuring the kin group respects the law and fulfills its obligations (1941: 70). Joyce describes this rank as magistrates, a not unfanciful analogy (1913: 158). The *fer fothlai* is a rich *bóaire* on the path to the status of nobility, as mentioned earlier. The other three grades are blurred somewhat but Binchy's glossary observes that the *mruig*fer* is the 'normal person' in Irish law for *Críth Gablach*, a role which the *bóaire* fills in most other tracts (1978: 78).

The *ócaire*, or 'young aire' is the lowest grade of freeman of full age and status recognised as a 'person' in Irish law (Binchy, 1941: 101). The 'young' (*óc-*) may refer to the age of this rank at the time of writing the law tracts, rather than the age of the person. Apparently what happened was that increased numbers of freemen made it difficult for all to secure the necessary property qualifications, and hence the jurists inserted a lower grade of commoner (1941: 102). This would have been a common-sense response to the conventional social problem of property division in the face of increasing population.

Non-free status

The unfree class consists of tenants-at-will. One class is the *fuidir* or 'semi-freeman', and Kelly notes that one law tract distinguishes no less than ten different types, although many of these distinctions are of little significance (1988: 33). A *fuidir* is free to quit the tenancy, subject to the law. But a *dóer*fuidir*, or 'base fuidir' may not exercise this right and has no independent legal status.

It might be expected that a 'cottier' or *bothach* would be beneath the *doer*fuidir* but this is not clear, despite the fact that such a class existed (Kelly 1988: 35). Finally, a *fuidir* or *bothach* whose forebears have occupied the same land for three generations, is reduced to the status of *senchléithe*, a class that is bound to the lord and cannot renounce the tenancy. Although not a slave, the *senchléithe* is sold with the land, which would make this group the equivalent of a serf class.

Finally, there is a slave class, whose members have no rights or legal existence whatever.

Conclusion

On the basis of the above analysis, the concept of status in early Irish society emerges as a logical consequence of the underlying philosophy on which society was based in the Indo-European culture. Social function ('holy' evolving into 'privileged'), land ownership and birth all played a complex but interrelated role in determining status.

What made the early Irish social system unique, however, was the additional concept of rank within the main grades. And it is this concept which, in turn, coloured the legal definition of rank by assigning an honour-price to each.

Viewed in the round, it was a stable social system, with the added advantage of mobility between the privileged and non-privileged, thereby ensuring internal renewal. It was an extraordinarily sophisticated system, which not only deserves wider appreciation but also a new multi-disciplinary approach to research from the academic community. The small number of references cited in this essay is proof that much more research needs to be done on status in early Irish society.

Chapter 3

Advice from a Princely in-Law:

the wisdom texts in Old Irish

Summary

Wisdom texts are defined in this essay as political advice or instructions given in early Irish society by a relative or tutor to a prospective or new king.

The texts are analysed in the context of Indo-European culture, which ascribed a sacral role to kings, who, in turn, embodied the communal prosperity and well-being of the people.

Nine texts traditionally regarded as part of the Speculum Principum genre of Old Irish literature are analysed from a political science perspective in terms of their central thrust, structure, form and content. It is concluded that only four of the texts conform with the definition specified, and that others belong to the category of proverbial wisdom.

The durability of the genre is examined by reference to early and late medieval Ireland, with the suggestion that the genre might have had a greater role in the native culture than that commonly accepted. It is recommended that this be made the subject of new research.

Introduction

Wisdom texts are a literary genre in early Irish consisting of formal political advice to a king in respect of personal conduct and the official discharge of his duties as a ruler. Known elsewhere as the *Speculum Principum/Principis* 'Mirror of princes/a prince' or *Fürstenspiegel*, and in Irish by a number of terms, of which *Tecosc(a)* [*Ríg*] 'Instruction(s) [of a king]' is the most representative, the genre is believed to have originated deep from within the prevailing culture.

One theory has it that these texts spring from the inauguration ceremonies at which kings were invested with authority. In other words, they are essentially derivative in nature.

Despite the antiquity of the inauguration ceremony, and despite its importance, no detailed account of its format in Irish society survives from the earliest period (Ó Corráin 1972: 35), but it seems that as part of the ceremony the *ollam* or chief poet of the dynasty sang the praises of the new king and recited his genealogy. The latter was the equivalent of a charter of rights and was proof of the king's title to reign (36). This conferred legitimacy on the new king, an essential feature of any political system.

Keating says in *Foras Feasa ar Éirinn* (Comyn and Dineen 1902-14: vol. 3, 10) that a *Teagasc Ríogh* was indeed read out at these inauguration ceremonies 'from the coming of Patrick ... to the Norman invasion', and he adds that the dynastic historian or *ollam* read aloud the *speculum principis* at the inauguration.

Notwithstanding some contemporary reservations about his credibility as a historian, I would take Keating as a reliable authority on social customs and rituals, especially as, in this case, he is corroborated by the well-known account by John le Fourdan recording the coronation of Alexander III of Scotland in the twelfth century, at which the laws and oaths relating to the king were read out to him (Kelly 1976: xiv).

More to the point, Dillon (1952) edited 'The story of the finding of Cashel' containing a *rosc* or rhetoric, after which the king says *rob fír fírthar, rob bríg brígther* 'may it be a truth which is fulfilled, may it be a power which is enforced'. The people respond to this 'Amen' (Kelly 1976: xiv). MacCana believes that the genre is traditional and preliterate and 'an integral part of the pagan liturgy of sovereignty' (1979: 448). This would seem to vindicate the idea that a traditional inauguration ceremony took place at which a druid or member of the learned class publicly recited a *speculum* to which the king expressed consent and which was then affirmed by the people.

On this basis, it is possible to reconstruct the inauguration ceremony into five parts: establishment of legitimacy by recounting the new king's genealogy; confirmation of his fitness to rule by reciting his personal prowess; swearing into office by reading a *speculum principis* or *tecosc*; taking of the oath of office and its affirmation by the people; and coronation or formal investiture by conferring a white rod as the symbol of authority, to which Keating makes reference.

Two indispensable elements of the ceremony were that it should take place at a site dedicated to that purpose and be followed by a *crechríg* or royal foray, 'by which the king demonstrated his suitability for office and acquired not only a heroic reputation but also the wealth in cattle to play a generous lord' (Ó Corráin 1972: 37), i.e. he demonstrated martial prowess and acquired the means for dispensing hospitality.

Viewed from this perspective, the wisdom texts would be basically literary compositions based on public ceremony, analogous in the Ireland of today to that of the swearing in of the president in accordance with the provisions of the constitution. It would not be too fanciful to argue that every society, no matter how primitive, has a constitution, or legal framework, for the exercise of authority and the imposition of duties and limits on those who exercise it, and that in early Irish society the inauguration ceremony was the occasion for the public reaffirmation of the 'constitution'.

Against this background, Ó Corráin encapsulates the first theory by arguing that the function of the *ollam* as ritual adviser to the king at the inauguration ceremony gave rise to the genre of *speculum principis* (1972: 36). Nevertheless, there is no evidence as to how or why the subject matter of established public ceremony was transformed into private literature as seen in the wisdom texts themselves. In the absence of such evidence, the theory is little more than speculation and, as will emerge later, would appear to be untenable.

The second theory is that advanced by Smith (1927), who characterised early Irish society as one which delighted in proverbs and sententious sayings. He noted that the literature from the period abounds in maxims and proverbial phrases which are not confined to random quotations since, 'whole collections of them ... are to be found in fairly old manuscripts' (1927: 411). He regarded the instructions to princes as one considerable subdivision of Irish sententious literature.

Smith later expanded on this theory by arguing (1930: 33) that there was no reason for believing any of the *tecosca* was composed by the persons whose names they bear. He offered two reasons for this conclusion. First, 'they are not the sort of writing expected from the pen of any individual'. He developed the second reason into what can be taken as his central thesis: 'instead, they would seem to represent the slow growth, anonymously, of popular proverbial literature, added to from generation to generation, and finally collected and classified by an industrious scribe'.

Later again, authorship was ascribed to kings and kingmakers noted for their wisdom in an attempt to invest them with dignity and authority. On this basis, the wisdom texts are the product of that ubiquitous character in medieval Ireland, the anonymous scribe of surpassing industry and devilish cunning, whose schemes are exposed by a sombre, street-wise scholar a millennium later.

This would place the genre more or less on par with other branches of proverbial wisdom, so that it was nothing more than a reflection of the prevailing common culture. As such, the content would mainly be of interest to the anthropologist. From a literary perspective, the *speculum/tecosc* would simply be an anthology of proverbs ordered in accordance with the preferences or whims of the collectors. This, too, seems untenable on the basis of the evidence emerging from a review of the genre.

McCone, by way of contrast, encapsulates the wisdom texts within his grander theory that all early Irish literature is the product of a Christian literati, ruthless reshapers of pagan tradition as he describes them. Within this global framework, the wisdom texts are said to have obvious affinities with Old Testament wisdom literature, because the monastic literati drew pertinent parallels between their gnomic literature and that of the Bible.

The question and answer format of the *Tecosca Cormaic* is allegedly derived from a monastic schoolroom and, anyway, is similar to Solomon's instructions to his son (1990: 31). He further believes (142) that it is no coincidence the three wisdom texts purporting to belong to the pre-Christian period in Ireland should be ascribed to early believers in Christianity and dismisses Smith's claim that they come from a purely pagan tradition. Instead, he argues, they contain little or nothing of that tradition.

This latter claim can be disputed by reference to the three texts, as will be seen below. At this point, it suffices to say that McCone's master-theory falls short as an explanation for the texts; it would reduce them to an incidental sideshow in an Orwellian conspiracy to rewrite history from top to bottom. Above all, it fails to take account of the fact that politics, irrespective of its cultural context, has enduring pre-occupations, one of them being that rulers should sleep easy in their beds (as Shakespeare reminds us).

But in advancing his theory, as mentioned earlier, Smith noted perceptively that the wisdom texts consist of instructions to princes 'given by their tutors or advisers, often by their fathers, whom they are about to succeed' (1927: 411). Meyer had immediately noted in his preface to *Tecosca Cormaic* that the instructions were 'given by princes to their heirs, by tutors to their disciples or by foster-fathers to their sons' (1909: v).

These insights allow for a fourth theory, since, in every case, the instructions are attributed to one individual and directed at another. In other words, they are personal in terms of their authorship, and equally so in terms of their intended audience. This specific characteristic would place the speculum principis in the realm of political science rather than see it as a reflection of ceremonial ritual, an example of accumulated proverbial wisdom or a sub-plot in rewriting early Irish history.

As in the case of Machiavelli's *The Prince*, the essential purpose of the wisdom text is political, and the aim is to prepare someone for the highest office and to advise them on how to hold onto it, i.e., such texts outline how a ruler should behave as a prince and how a prince should behave as a ruler. The instructor is older and wiser than the instructed and, as Meyer and Smith observed, related to him by blood, marriage or fosterage. The wisdom text might be described as the wisdom of the in-laws; certainly it can be called the wisdom of the insiders.

The concept of kingship

The theory that a *speculum principis* is consciously intended as advice to a prospective or new king on kingly behaviour gains force from the very concept of kingship in early Irish society. As Ó Corráin has explained (1972: 42) the king was a sacred personage, and through the rule of the rightful king nature was fertile and fruitful. Society flourished and peace reigned. On the other hand, an unjust king brought war, famine, unrest and death on his people – the four horsemen of the Apocalypse rode the land. The king was thus not just a political and military figure but, more importantly, a priestly personage who embodied the people. Their fortunes and prosperity rested on his personal behaviour and the public conduct of his office.

Given the pivotal importance of agriculture in pastoral societies, and given also the utter dependence of agricultural economies on the vagaries of nature for the supply of food, the communal instinct to appease nature was a common sense approach to collective self-protection. Indeed, the societal instinct in early Ireland, and many other similar societies, was to go beyond appeasing nature and, instead, turn it into an ally; more than that, in fact, the specific intent of the inauguration ceremony was to make nature an ally by marriage. For that reason, the king married the goddess of the territory and the ceremony was a sacred marriage between the two, which as late as 1310 was described as a king-marriage (Ó Corráin, 1972: 33). Indeed, Kelly views the relationship between a king and his territory in sexual terms when he quotes from the same source, the *Annals of Connacht*, which describe the inauguration of Fedlimid as his 'sleeping with the province of Connacht' (*feis re cóiced* Connacht, Kelly 1988: 18).

To fulfil his role as the protector of the people, the king not only had to be without physical blemish, but also without spiritual imperfection, i.e. he had to be a perfect consort for the goddess. Physical perfection was easily discerned (and there are many examples where any disfigurement through the loss of a limb or damage to other body-parts leads to immediate abdication). But spiritual imperfection is not so easily detected; it usually emerges over time through conduct and requires constant vigilance by the people to prevent it, and vigorous self-discipline by the king to avoid it. This would explain the emphasis in the wisdom texts on the overriding necessity for the king to be always true to his calling, i.e. at all times, in every place, and in each circumstance, to be a man of the truth.

In the law texts, many crimes and omissions on the part of the king are regarded as breaches of his justice and can lead to his overthrow (Kelly 1988: 18). His honour-price would be lost if he defaulted on his oath or tolerated satire (15). Thus, the king must be wise, valorous and just if he is to be a true king, i.e. the protector of the people he personifies, the one who literally embodies their concordat with nature and guarantees their survival and prosperity. In short, the king is the living truth, a prospect at which modern politicians would blanch.

Nature of the wisdom texts

In his famous lecture, 'The archaism of Irish tradition', delivered in 1947, Dillon drew parallels between the Hindu and Irish belief in the magic power of the truth by referring to sagas in both traditions (1947: 247–50). He quoted a poem in the *Book of Leinster*, which says that in respect of a prince the three best things for him during his reign are 'truth, mercy and silence', and then went on to repeat the sacral role of the prince, for 'a prince's truth is an effort which overpowers armies: it brings milk into the world, it brings corn and mast' (250).

The magic power of the truth comes across as the most fundamental theological or ideological belief which explains the universe by means of an ordered harmony between the gods of the other world and humankind. Any breach of that harmony by a disavowal or betrayal of the truth brings immediate retribution, not only on those responsible but also on others; in the case of the prince, it spells disaster for the people as a whole. Ó Cathasaigh says that this concept is found in the laws and the sagas and testifies to an anthropocentric world-view which pervades the Irish literature on kingship: the king is the centre of the cosmos (1972: 64–5).

Hence, the singular importance of the prince being faithful to the truth, particularly in respect of maintaining harmony within society, i.e. ensuring that justice is done. The pivotal task for the prince is, consequently, to be the fountainhead of justice. Through him, justice flows like water through a conduit, a metaphor justified by the Hindu belief that Truth was localised in a huge lake at the summit of heaven (Dillon 1947: 250) and by the Irish belief in the sacredness of the River Boyne.

This representation of the cosmos explains the central role assigned to the prince as the interface between men and gods and, consequently, the unrelenting emphasis in the inauguration ceremony and in the wisdom texts on the utter necessity for the prince to act in accordance with the truth by being just. In practical terms this meant, above all, that the king had to make true judgements in the everyday discharge of his duties – otherwise the house would literally fall down, as it began to do when Lugaid Mac Con gave a false judgement, only for Cormac to stay the house by pronouncing a true verdict (Kelly 1969: 4).

This insight into the overwhelming power and importance of the truth and the king's role as its guardian and protector puts the wisdom texts in their true context, i.e. the native ideology of kingship (Ó Cathasaigh, 1972: 65) rather than a hybrid of the Judaeo-Christian tradition, as McCone would have it.

It should be added, of course, that ideology, theology or religious belief is only one dimension to human behaviour. There are other more unworthy concerns in the realm of politics in which any prince had to operate. Caesar was, after all, both *Pontifex Maximus* and a military dictator.

Consequently, the wisdom texts will be found to be a complex mixture of advice on religion (as defined above), power, politics, human nature and the art of survival, mixing the trivial with the exalted, the particular with the universal, and the philanthropic with self-interest.

Primary sources

In the preface to his translation of *Tecosca Cormaic* (1909), the great German scholar, Kuno Meyer, provided a list of the wisdom texts as follows:

- *Audacht Morainn*
- *Bríatharthecosc Con Culainn*
- *Senbríathra* or *Senráite Fíthail*
- *Sayings of Flann Fína*
- *Tecosca Cormaic*

At that point, *Audacht Morainn* had neither been edited nor translated. The *Bríatharthecosc Con Culainn* had, on the other hand, been edited by Windisch and translated four times.

But the *Senbríathra Fíthail* had not been edited or translated, and neither had the sayings of *Flann Fína*. As for the *Tecosca Cormaic*, Meyer had offered the first publication and translation of the entire text (1909), and so launched the genre on what should have been a sea of scholarship, but which has proven to be a shallow pool, mostly stagnant.

In his introduction to *Audacht Morainn*, three quarters of a century later, Kelly (1976: xiii) says the *Speculum Principum* genre is represented by the following five texts, all of which had, by then, been both edited and translated:

- *Audacht Morainn*
- *Tecosca Cormaic*
- *Bríatharthecosc Con Culainn*
- *Tecosc Cuscraid*
- *Senbríathra Fíthail*

Kelly offers no explanation for limiting the list to this number or for the order chosen, other than to note that the text he has edited, *Audacht Morainn*, is the earliest of this group; grammar, orthography and syntax pointing to a date c. ad 700.

Over a decade later he expanded his list on the basis that the wisdom texts are 'particularly useful in that they contain some general statements expressing early Irish views on the society's structure and ethos' (1988: 2). In addition to the five texts quoted above, he included *Trechend Breth Féne*, translated by Meyer (1906) under the title *The Triads of Ireland*, and the *Aibidil Luigne maic Éremóin*, edited and translated by Smith (1928a) as *Aibidil Cuigne maic Emoin* (on which, see Kelly 1988: 286).

R.M. Smith, the American scholar who specialised during the 1920s in the *Speculum Principum*, and haunted the Trinity College library, provided a more elaborate listing and also offered two sets of classification, the first based on the importance and popularity of a text, the second dividing the texts into the periods to which they can be assigned.

Quite properly, he warns that it would be impossible to trace any of the *Tecosca*, as he calls them, to their original sources or to say how soon they were given literary form (1927: 413). All that can be said, he argues, is that they had their origin at some time between the period to which they are traditionally assigned and the period, spanning perhaps several centuries, of the language of the existing versions.

On that basis, he believes that both the *Audacht Morainn* and the *Tecosca Cormaic* must have been popular well before the beginning of the ninth century and goes on to say that 'the pagan character which the originals must have exhibited would seem to point to a date not far removed from the fifth century' (1927: 414).

He offers the following more extensive listing and orders it on the basis of the traditional assignment of the texts, *not* to be equated under any circumstances with date of composition (1927: 414):

First Century
- *Audacht Morainn*
- *Bríatharthecosc Con Culainn*
- *Tecosc Cuscraid*

Third Century
- *Tecosca Cormaic*
- *Senbríathra Fíthail*
- *Aibidil Luigne maic Éremóin*

Seventh and Eighth Centuries
- *Briathra Flainn *Fína*
- Poem ascribed to St Moling

Aside from the traditional basis for dating the origin of the wisdom texts, Smith justifies his division by referring to the distinct characteristics of each group. The first-century group is more archaic and obscure in meaning; in form it consists of rugged rhythmical prose, while in style it is marked by recurrent alliteration, tmesis and parataxis.

The third-century group is most characterised by the striking trait of a regular formula, from which the text seldom departs. In contrast to the first-century group, the form and style are simple but the use of a fixed formula leads to extreme regularity and a terseness of expression, sometimes to the point of unintelligibility.

The third group, from the seventh and eighth centuries, shows a Christian influence, unlike its predecessors, and lacks their primitive vigour. Nevertheless, this group borrows phraseology from the other two and imitates them in other respects (1927: 414–15).

Smith appears to be the only scholar to have made a systematic study of the genre as a whole (while also editing some of the above texts), and his criteria for classification merit particular respect. As will be seen, his judgements and analysis are not always well grounded, but his framework for listing the wisdom texts is still acceptable in the absence of anything better.

Finally, it is worth noting that Smith regards the *Audacht Morainn*, the *Tecosca Cormaic* and the *Senbríathra Fíthail* as the most prominent of the texts not only for the number of copies that have come down to us but also because they are often found together in older manuscripts and only rarely are found to stand alone in any manuscript (1927: 412). Using Smith's historical classification, the various texts are analysed below in chronological order from the perspective of political advice to a potential or actual king.

Audacht Morainn

Audacht means 'bequest' or 'legacy' or 'testament', and its use in the title of this first text is appropriate to the context in which the advice is transmitted. Morann is on his deathbed and describes what he has to say as *mo bríathra rem bás,* 'my words before my death'.

According to the *Annals of the Four Masters,* Morann was son of Cairbre Cinn Chait, who usurped the throne of Ireland after the vassal tribes had destroyed the nobility. The rightful heir, Feradach, assumed the kingship after Cairbre's disastrous reign and appointed Morann his chief judge (Smith 1927: 415). Now on the point of death, Morann instructs his foster-son Neire to convey the testament to Feradach.

The significance of the wisdom imparted is that Morann was famed as a judge, revered for his wisdom and devotion to justice and acknowledged for centuries afterwards as a most authoritative jurist and commentator on the laws.

More particularly, his advice to Feradach is dispassionate and disinterested, dedicated no doubt to ensuring that order and harmony are completely restored after the chaos for which he must feel some element of guilt.

In other words, the Testament is the distillation of the accumulated wisdom of the wisest of judges and has an intensely practical political purpose, i.e. that Feradach should be a just king, and hence successful. As argued earlier, *Audacht Morainn* is personal communication, although delivered through a trusted intermediary, and is neither an account of ceremonial ritual, nor an anthology of proverbial wisdom nor a Christian polemic.

The *Audacht Morainn* (AM) was first edited by Thurneysen (1917). The text edited by Kelly (1976) was established by Dr Binchy, in a seminar he conducted in 1963, from RIA manuscript 23 N.10, which was transcribed in 1575 but preserves most of the archaic spellings (Kelly 1976: xxv). Thurneysen had earlier concluded that AM derived from the famous missing manuscript, *Cín Dromma Snechtai*, generally dated to the early-eighth century (Kelly 1976: xxvi).

All in all, there are seven witnesses extant, found, *inter alia*, in the twelfth-century *Book of Leinster*, the fourteenth-century *Yellow Book of Lecan* and the fifteenth-century TCD manuscript *H 2.7*, as well as the sixteenth-century RIA manuscript mentioned above (Kelly 1976: xxvi).

Kelly believes, on the basis of a number of archaic spellings, best preserved in the text edited by him, that it 'was written down well before the main Würzburg glosses', and that this gives us a compilation date of approximately ad 700, though much of the text 'must have had a previous oral or possibly manuscript existence' (xxix). Archaic features of syntax, however, suggested to him that much of his recension was composed a good deal earlier than the proposed compilation date of c. ad 700 (xxxiii –xl).

An analysis of the text in terms of content suggests that AM can be divided into at least eight parts:

		Paras
(1)	Introduction	1-5
(2)	Maxims on justice	6-21
(3)	Precepts for a young King	22
(4)	More maxims on justice	23-29
(5)	Advice on how to rule	30-52
(6)	Proverbial wisdom	53-54
(7)	Instructions on becoming a true ruler	55-62
(8)	Conclusion	63

The introduction opens with a brief explanation of the background to the *Audacht*, which is editorial in style. It then continues in what purports to be Morann's own words, instructing Neire to bring his dying words to Feradach, his lasting advice as he describes it.

In part two, the *Audacht* immediately sets out a series of maxims on justice, which corresponds exactly with the sacral role of the king outlined above. That justice (*fír flathemon* in the text) is chosen for the opening section merely reinforces its fundamental importance in the role assigned to the king. 'Let him preserve justice, it will care for him' (§6). 'It is through the justice of the ruler that he secures peace, tranquillity, joy, ease, comfort' (§14). 'It is through the justice of the ruler that abundances of great tree-fruit of the great wood are tasted' (§17).

Part three consists of a brief interpolation, which is best understood as advice from a wise counsellor to a new ruler and is simply an attempt to put an old head on young shoulders. Part four resumes the maxims on justice, although more in a practical than a philosophical vein. Part five reverts to personal advice, being a series of guidelines on how to rule wisely, ranging from maintaining peace – 'bloodshed is a vain destruction of all rule' (§29) – to the regulation of business affairs, the administration of the laws and the maintenance of social stability.

What follows next might seem out of place, for it consists, as Smith would have it, of proverbial wisdom. There are thirteen proverbs in all, the tenor of which is that everything changes and certain things are inevitable. The overall thrust is stoic, without any reference to Christian belief and can be justified as the philosophic setting for the next section, which is the most profound passage in the *Audacht*: fifteen virtues of a good ruler are expounded and ten things which extinguish justice are enumerated (§§55, 56).

Four types of ruler are described in this section; the true, the wily, the occupier and the tyrant (§§58–62). The king is reminded stoically that he will die (*memento mori*). How he will be remembered will depend on how he practised or ignored the virtues of just kingship during his life (§57).

The text concludes with a refrain from the introduction: the underlying motivation of Morann in bestowing his wisdom on Feradach is the protection of his own kin. Unquestionably, this confirms that the primary purpose of the *Audacht* is to ensure social stability as a direct consequence of just rule by a king who abides by 'truth'.

As political advice to a prince, it could hardly be bettered as a reflection on the transitory nature of power and glory (*sic transit gloria mundi*) and an admonition in purely human terms as to why he should be a true ruler: 'he whom the living do not glorify with blessings is not a true ruler' (§59).

At the same time, *AM* perfectly welds the power of the truth to more human or mundane considerations: 'the true ruler smiles on the truth when he hears it, he exalts it when he sees it'. Power, politics and religion are married with elegance and precision into a message that cannot be misunderstood, at least not by an actual ruler.

Bríatharthecosc Con Culainn

The saga *Serglige Con Culainn* ('The wasting sickness of Cú Chulainn') contains an episode in which Cú Chulainn gives advice to Lugaid Réo nDerg, who has been chosen to be king of Tara. The only extant copies of the story have come down to us in *Lebor na hUidre* (twelfth century) and TCD H 4. 22, possibly from the seventeenth century (Dillon 1953: xi).

The text is a mixture of two recensions which, Dillon believes, come from the ninth century and the twelfth century, respectively (xiii). Dillon edited the Trinity College manuscript copy in 1949 and translated it in 1953 (Dillon 1949 and 1953a, respectively). In the same year he edited the text contained in *Lebor na hUidre* (Dillon 1953).

Dillon believes that this collection of *tecosca* is an interruption in the wider story of Cú Chulainn's foray into the otherworld and can hardly belong to the original version (1953: x). Smith (1925) had already translated the section containing the instructions, arguing that the content had not yet been given the discussion it merited.

He pointed out that the 'writer's familiarity with ancient Irish law, and his familiarity with earlier compositions of the "instructions" type, notably the *Tecosca Cormaic*' were worthy of note (1925: 187).

Knowledge of the *Tecosca Cormaic* was attested not only by resemblances in general vocabulary, but by insertions of complete lines from that composition (1925: 187). Obviously, this analysis conflicts with Smith's later classification of the *Tecosca* by period, a point which he does not explain and which is beyond the competence of this writer to unravel.

The 'instructions' section, despite being regarded as a later addition by Dillon, seems to fit quite naturally in the narrative. While Cú Chulainn is suffering from the wasting sickness, the four provinces of Ireland are meeting in Tara to choose a king in order to fill a seven-year vacuum left by the death of Conaire. The successor is identified in a vision following a bull-feast as 'a young warrior, noble and strong, with two red circles around his body, standing over the pillow of a sick man in Emuin' (1953: 56).

When approached by messengers from Tara seeking such a man, Conchobar identifies him as Lugaid Réo nDerg, who fortuitously happens to be close by 'comforting his foster-father, Cú Chulainn, who is sick'. On hearing this, and as Lugaid prepares to depart for Tara, Cú Chulainn immediately issues his instructions to the putative king. The two manuscript versions of the saga correspond almost exactly, and both confirm the thesis that the *tecosca* consist of personal political advice from an older counsellor to a young prince, in this instance from a foster-father to a foster-son, perhaps the closest of personal relationships in early Irish society.

The content of *Serglige Con Culainn* cannot be so easily divided as that in the *Audacht Morainn*, since the former consists of only two categories of instructions, which might be termed princely behaviour and respect for the law, and both are intertwined in the short text. The most striking feature of the instructions, however, is their urgency; they are short, sharp admonitions without any philosophical framework or any resort to proverbial wisdom, still less to religion. The tone is paternal, as befits the relationship, and the instructions are mainly given in the negative, thus emphasising their urgency. Lugaid is told of things not to do, thereby avoiding those pitfalls that bring down a ruler through unjust or unacceptable behaviour.

There are thirty instructions relating to princely behaviour in the TCD manuscript, of which only four are cast in the positive (1953a: 57–8). They range from the essentially political – 'seek out not men of ill fame and little power' to the intensely personal – 'do not play the buffoon, do not mock'. There is emphasis on the value of advice from the wise and the old; on the benefit of being cautious and generous; and on the need to be stern towards enemies and warm towards friends; above all, the advice is not to be too garrulous, contentious or vulgar.

The same manuscript contains ten legal maxims, which corroborate Smith's judgement on Cú Chulainn's knowledge of the law, and which doubtless gladdened the hearts of contemporary lawyers. While separated by intervening instructions, they constitute an organic whole centered around the primacy of contracts and the importance of established jurisprudence. Only one refers to justice *per se*, yet it is pregnant with wisdom: justice must not be suppressed in the face of public pressure, i.e. it is better to be just than to be popular. Lugaid immediately responds that it would be well for every man to know these instructions and promises that he will abide by them. On going to Tara, he is proclaimed king and reigns for twenty-seven years.

Despite their brevity, the *tecosca* in *Serglige Con Culainn* consist of eminently sensible advice from a man who knows how the political world works, understands human nature and values order in society. That they lack the philosophical framework of a jurist like Morann is hardly surprising, but then the *Audacht* lacks the sharpness expected of a man of action. The passage, as said earlier, seems to fall naturally into the flow of the narrative and gives an insight into the character of Cú Chulainn, which is invaluable in arriving at a rounded view of his personality. He is more than a great warrior; he is also reflective, wise and educated – as well as being an articulate counsellor who knows what it takes to operate in the world of politics.

Tecosc Cuscraid

The primary sources for the *Tecosc Cuscraid*, according to Best (1916: 170), are the Book of Lecan and the sixteenth century TCD manuscript, *H 3.18*. His translation of the *Book of Lecan* recension appeared in 1916 under the title 'The Battle of Airtech'. Smith seemed unaware of this version, despite referring to Best, when he claimed there was only one text to hand, adding that it was very corrupt (1927:

421). For this and other reasons he doubted its reliability, although he had no hesitation in using it.

On the other hand, Best thought that the *Cath Airtig*, in which the *tecosca* appear, was a natural sequel to the *Bruiden Dá Chocae*, as it filled a gap in the Conchubar-Cú Chulainn cycle. He also thought the *tecosca* to be an example of the instruction given to a newly elected prince, 'which would seem to have been part of an inauguration ceremony' (1916: 170), although in the narrative the *tecosca* seem to follow the ceremony rather than be part of it.

The background to the tale provides the context for this particular wisdom text. After the death of Conchubar and that of his son, Cormac, before he was even proclaimed king, the Ulstermen offer the kingdom to Conall Cernach who refuses it on the grounds that the responsibilities are too great for him (Smith 1927: 421). He recommends that his foster-son, Cuscraid, also a natural son of Conchobar, be appointed instead.

Thereupon, Cuscraid is proclaimed king and it is then that Conall speaks, indicating that his intervention is a spontaneous reaction to events, like Cú Chulainn's, rather than a measured deliberate message, like that of Morann, or of Cormac as will be seen below. In fact, Conall first laments the loss of Conchubar, his mighty sovereign (without mentioning Cormac at all), and he is so stricken with grief that he wants to die. Only then does he utter his instructions to the man who has just become Conchubar's successor.

The instructions are short and to the point, there being only ten in all. It is utterly clear that they are a personal communication between an older man and a new king. As in the case of Cú Chulainn and Lugaid, the relationship is that of foster-father and foster-son. The fact that the instructions are given in public does not detract from the immediacy or intimacy of the communication, and so this example fits with the theory about wisdom texts offered at the outset.

There are only ten instructions given by Conall, all but one expressed positively, and again it is too difficult to divide such a short text into logically coherent elements. The better approach is to focus on themes. Not unexpectedly, Cuscraid is told to be just and righteous in judgement and to be a follower of the sovereign law, thereby reaffirming the sacral role of the king. Continuing this theme, he is advised to fulfill oaths and to consolidate the law of his rule, i.e. to be faithful to the truth, lest his misdeeds bring ruin on the people.

A political theme, not so clearly evident in the *Audacht Morainn* and hardly present in the *Briatharthecosc Con Culainn*, is developed with reference to the advisability of holding frequent assemblies for resolving border disputes and appeasing the nobility. This is repeated in an instruction to protect the territory by ardent and warlike means in contending with 'foreign lands'. But, in this regard, Cuscraid is advised against going to war too hastily, lest it add unnecessarily to sorrow.

Finally, the theme of appropriate princely behaviour is developed. Apart from a warning not to be drunk in a pub (a common theme in the *tecosca*), the new king is shrewdly advised to be well-briefed, or multi-lingual as it is put, for fear that he would appear ignorant in public on any topic.

The implication is that being outsmarted in public would detract from his aura of authority.

For all its brevity, the *Tecosca Cuscraid* contains the main political points that any counsellor would wish to get across to a new and untried king, in this case one who is not only taking office in a crisis but who is also an intimate relation. From this perspective, the task is fulfilled admirably. Moreover, what is said adds greatly to our understanding of kingship at the time of the *Táin*, as it is in harmony with the instructions in the *Audacht* and the *Bríatharthecosc Con Chulainn*.

Tecosca Cormaic

If Cú Chulainn and Conall Cernach were mercifully short, and Morann brief and precise, neither of these traits can be said to be true of Cormac, son of Art, son of Conn, the greatest and wisest of Irish kings, whose reign ended in 266. His *Tecosc Ríg* runs to 48 pages of small print and practically covers every conceivable aspect of kingship; it is virtually impossible to summarise adequately in an essay and deserves a book in itself. *The Instructions of Cormac* were first published and translated in their entirety by the eminent scholar Kuno Meyer (1909), and he was convinced that the form in which the text has come down to us was compiled during the Old Irish period of the language, not later than the first half of the ninth century as far as he could judge from numerous verbal forms (1909: xi). For this reason, Ó Cathasaigh, in assessing Cormac's heroic biography, says that the attribution belongs to tradition rather than history (1972: 86).

The background to the *Tecosc Ríg* is given in the *Book of Aicill* which tells us that after Cormac had been deprived of one of his eyes by Áengus he retired to Aicill, and the sovereignty of Ireland passed to his son Cairbre Lifechair. When faced with a difficult case for judgement Cairbre was wont to go for advice to his father, and the continuous interchange between the two led to the compilation of the *tecosca* (Smith, 1927: 428).

Keating gives a similar explanation for the background to the text, adding that the *Tecosc Ríg* set forth 'what a king should be...and how he should rule the people through their laws' (Comyn and Dinneen, 1902–14, vol. 2: 347).

The *Tecosca Cormaic* is by far the longest treatise on politics in Old Irish literature. It is structured in the form of questions and answers, a style which McCone had attributed to the influence of the monastic schoolroom. The questions put by Cairbre are terse and to the point, giving little flavour of his personality, although here and there a psychologist could detect some interesting traits. Essentially, he is an instrument for Cormac to expound on a political topic of his own choosing.

The answers follow no set formula in terms of style or length, varying from some short pithy responses of one line to fairly lengthy dissertations on a theme. There is a page and a half in respect of the proper qualities of a king, and nearly four pages on women, in what is hardly a feminist credo and which McCone aptly calls a 'great misogynist litany' (1990: 77).

Thematically, the instructions do not progress systematically through the role, nature and responsibilities of kingship but shift from the general to the particular in no observable pattern. Neither do they offer the sort of philosophic overview that lends a certain solemnity to the *Audacht Morainn*, and there are no reflections on life as a passing vale of sorrows. The stoicism of Morann is absent. So too are references to Christian belief. While God is mentioned occasionally, it is only in passing and obviously added as a scribal after-thought.

But, on the other hand, the instructions provide a profound psychological insight into human nature, its strengths and weaknesses, its follies and triumphs. Their greatest value to a prince is, as a result, Cormac's advice on how to govern. This would be at odds with the background presented by the *Book of Aicill* and by Keating, if both are to be taken as suggesting that Cairbre was seeking advice from his father when faced with a difficult legal problem, but would be entirely consistent with the implication that the judgements Cairbre had to make were essentially political, i.e. to do with kingcraft rather than adjudication; this would seem to be the better representation of the main thrust of the *Instructions*.

From a thematic perspective, the lengthy text can be divided into the following topics, bearing in mind that there is no consistency in paragraph length:

	Thematic Division	Paras
1.	Requirements for success	1
2.	Duties	2
3.	Rules of good governance	3
4.	Responsibilities of his steward	4

	Thematic Division	**Paras**
5.	Accession to power	5
6.	Proper qualities of a king	6
7.	Preparation for office	7-8
8.	Lessons from life	9-10
9.	Advice on princely behaviour	11-12
10.	Reflections on human nature	13
11.	The ways of folly	14-15
12.	On women	16
13.	Proverbial wisdom	17-18
14.	Rules on personal behaviour	19
15.	Proverbial wisdom	20-21
16.	Legal maxims	22-24
17.	Political maxims	25-26
18.	People to avoid	27-28
19.	Rules for behaviour	29-31
20.	Pitfalls	32-33
21.	Personal staff	34
22.	Proverbial wisdom	35-37

This analysis suggests that the *Tecosca* can be grouped initially into 22 parts. A modern editor might impose a more rigorous order by rearranging them as follows for reasons of coherence:

	Restructured Text	**Paras**
1.	**Kingship**	
	Preparation	7-8
	Requirements for success	1
	Duties	5
	Demeanour	30

	Restructured Text	Paras
2.	**The Person**	
	Necessary qualities	6
	Princely behaviour	11-12
	Precautions	29
	Staff	4.34
3.	**The Ruler**	
	Ground rules	19
	Governance	3
	Politics	25-26
	Law	22-24
4.	**Human Nature**	
	Universal truths	13.31
	Weaknesses	14-15
	Ill Nature	27-28
	Personality Types	32-33
5.	**Proverbial Wisdom**	
	Life's lessons	9-10
	On women	16
	Good health	21
	Home truths	17-18
	Durability	20
	Final thoughts	35-37

If Cormac were to permit a textual rearrangement along these lines, the text would take on a greater coherence, and even though his consent cannot be secured at this distance it can be assumed for purposes of thematic analysis. Because the text is so long, the analysis itself will have to be impressionistic; a more detailed examination (mercifully) awaits another day.

The theme of kingship is opened in this new arrangement with preparations for the office. The two paragraphs presenting this topic are based on questions relating to Cormac's own youth. In enumerating his habits as a young man, all carefully designed to cultivate a reputation for maturity and shrewdness, he adds that 'it is through those habits that the young become old and kingly warriors' (§7.27).

Ó Cathasaigh laments the absence of legendary episodes in what he regards as a reply set in general terms (1972: 60). Indeed it is. It is intended as advice on how to behave before assuming power, not as an autobiographical account of princely heroics. No doubt, Henry V could have benefited from this advice, rather than consorting with Falstaff. The requirements for success, which actually open the text itself in a paragraph of 46 lines, contain all the by now familiar enjoinders about truth and justice, but add new advice about enriching society. A Christian influence is evident through two perfunctory references to God. Indeed, the conclusion to the paragraph asserts 'it is through the truth of a ruler that God gives all that', i.e. peace and abundance. But these sentiments are pious additions to the text and in no way affect its otherwise pagan provenance.

The requirements for assuming office are spelled out in a short paragraph (§ 5), but manage to compress ten qualifications into a clear definition of what it takes to make a king. Having entered office, the duties are explained in a long paragraph of 27 lines, in what are described as 'the duties of a lord towards tribes' (§2.31). It can be inferred that a higher king is in mind for the expression *fri túatha* is used in the original Irish. It needs to be said at once that the duties, although fearsome, have the common theme of consolidating peace, planting law, protecting the just, pursuing justice and bringing everyone under the law. There is a democratic twist to these sentiments that suggests there was much more to early Irish society than some historians have realised. There is meat here for some young hungry political scientist.

The section on kingship closes with a reply to a question: how should Cairbre behave. The qualities described are essentially those regarding the demeanour a king should adopt in a variety of circumstances. 'Be proud with the proud lest anyone make you tremble' (§30.4) gives a good flavour of the political advice on offer.

The second section, on the personality of the king, opens with one of the longest paragraphs (51 lines), in answer to the question: what are the proper qualities of a leader. In this case, the qualities expressed, for 23 lines, follow a formula of *rop* 'let him be' plus an adjective. After an interruption, the *rop* formula is resumed but, this time, with a phrase. The break in the pattern suggests two or more authors at work sometime before the present manuscript compilation, and if the material was copied directly from the *Cín Dromma Snechtai*, then the original composition would be very early indeed.

That said, the paragraph defies brief analysis. It does, however, repeat some of the duties as qualities, e.g. 'let him love truth, let him give true judgements', and contains a complex mixture of politics – 'let him be attended by few in secret councils' – ethics and even the social graces, plus short references to the need for a social conscience.

On princely behaviour (§§11 and 12), the first rule of thumb is that it's better to be sure than sorry, i.e. don't start what cannot be finished properly, for such failures 'are a crime in the gatherings of the world' (§11.14). The second is about those qualities which are 'hateful before God and man' (§12.18) in the public conduct of the prince, and which are to be avoided at all cost.

To these are added in paragraph 29 a second set of undesirable personality traits, which, in the end, focus on how to avert unreasonable expectations in the public mind or how to avoid being overthrown by enemies. These are precautionary in tone and full of political common sense; interestingly, each precept consists of opposites which are later explained in terms of their consequences – 'be not too harsh, you will be broken; if you be too feeble, you will be crushed' (§29.9, §29.16–17).

This section on the king's personality could be said to conclude with two paragraphs which are widely separated in the text (§§4 and 34), but which, in dealing with the matter of personal staff, come straight out of a Human Resources Manager's manual. The message is simple: do not put square pegs in round holes; surround yourself with those best fitted for the task assigned.

The third section has been called 'The ruler', and in

many ways is the core of the *speculum* for it concentrates on the very stuff of kingcraft. Paragraph 19, which runs to a page, can be regarded as the basic ground rules for a ruler. Although it is one of the few answers without any indication of the question, the theme is clearly related to success as a king. A notable feature of the paragraph is that all the instructions are cast in the negative, thus aping Cú Chulainn's advice to Lugaid. Essentially, the king is to be above the herd and to act as a unifying force in society, i.e. 'be not the laughing stock in an assembly' (§19.13) and 'do not be a leader in strife' (§19.19).

Paragraphs 25 and 26, here described as relating to politics, are both short, but to the point. Paragraph 25 specifically relates to what could be called parliamentary behaviour, as it answers a question about the worst form of arguing before an assembly, with the best form of argument to be understood by implication. The advice can be summed up in the precept that 'playing a dangerous game' (§25.10) is bad politics, i.e. don't take unjustifiable risks. Similarly, in paragraph 26, the worst practice in pleading is briefly summarised, and the tone of the advice can be caught in the belief being expressed that 'violence in discussion' and 'discussion without reason' are bad for debate, maxims that might be repeated on occasion with advantage by the Ceann Comhairle in the Dáil.

Finally, three paragraphs (§§22–24), can be characterised as advising the new king in the discharge of his judicial functions by warning him to be vigilant against certain types of pleading. These could be called guidelines for detecting bad evidence, and might be of interest to the distinguished chairmen of various tribunals.

Inevitably, *Cormac's Instructions* include long dissertations on the vagaries of human nature, and as expected of an old man who has seen it all, the message has all to do with weaknesses, follies, deceit and sharp practice. In the thematic restructuring of the text proposed here, these are gathered together from a number of paragraphs, which have been reassembled as Section 4. While they make for a woeful reading, e.g. 'everyone is a friend until it comes to debts' (§31.4), they are lightened by Cormac's descriptions of personality types in paragraphs 32 and 33.

While relatively short, these paragraphs are profound; the first describes those most open to ridicule, and hence to be shunned, and the second those likely to be the least dependable when it matters most, and hence to be avoided. A modern psychologist would hardly disagree with any of the conclusions. Thus fortified against the worst types in society, the new king can set off on his career clad in the invaluable armoury of what could be called Cormac's cynicism.

The concluding section draws together the sort of proverbial wisdom to which Smith has referred. In one sense, this is out of place, since some of Cormac's observations are those that could be heard in a country pub late at night, such as paragraph 17 on the weather, and 18 on housekeeping. Then again, some could be justified as practical advice, such as paragraph 21 on maintaining good health (*mens sana in corpore sano*). And the three closing paragraphs could be excused as the final ruminations on life, with Cairbre acting as an early Gay Byrne.

Paragraph 16, however, running to nearly four pages of vituperation against women, genuinely seems at odds with the purpose and tone of the instructions. It is also at odds with the answer to the question that prompts it:, what is the sweetest thing Cormac has heard (§10). He gives three replies, the last of which is 'a lady's invitation to her pillow' (§10.6). This would seem a truer reflection of his views, especially as it is counterpoised with his answer in the previous paragraph to the question as to the worst thing he has ever seen. In this case there is only one reply: 'faces of foes in a battle field' (§9.3). The contrast between the best and the worst could not be starker, or more human. For the sake of feminist well-being, and Cormac's reputation, the treatise on women is best left aside.

All that said, *Tecosca Cormaic* is as profound a piece of political advice as a new king could desire and is of enduring value to politicians, whatever their circumstances. It has suffered in three respects.

First, its structure seems haphazard; the absence of a good editor greatly weakens the force of what is a remarkable dissertation on the art of ruling. Second, despite its continuing popularity in medieval Ireland and the emergence of what could be called the 'Cult of Cormac', it disappeared more or less from the mainstream of European political thought, a fate it shared with many other Irish writings for reasons best left unsaid. Last, it has virtually gone ignored since Meyer published the text and its translation. *Cormac's Instructions* deserved better than this.

There is a book to be written yet that would restore it to its rightful place in the history of Irish and European political thought. It is immaterial whether Cormac wrote it or not. What can be said with confidence is that the *Instructions* represent Irish political thought around ad 700 at the latest, and are testimony to the culture of our early society. That is their real value. It should be realised.

Senbríathra Fíthail

Smith's theory, it will be recalled, was that the *Tecosca* were no more than 'popular proverbial literature' (1930: 33). If that theory has any validity, then certainly the *Senbríathra Fíthail* (*SF*) would be its strongest corroboration. Ascribed to Fíthal, the chief brehon of Cormac, and reputed to be a jurist as distinguished as Morann, the text is truly an anthology of sententious sayings, as its title suggests.

With the exception of one section, the text lacks the questions and answers structure evident in the *Audacht Morainn* and *Tecosca Cormaic*, has no ostensible purpose in mind and assuredly does not purport to be political advice to a prince. As such, it fails to meet the criteria laid down by Smith and others for being included in the genre of *Speculum Principum*.

In short, *Senbríathra Fíthail* is similar to O'Rahilly's *A miscellany of Irish proverbs* (1922), to which Smith acknowledged his indebtedness when editing and translating the *Senbríathra* text (1928: 3). There is a complication, however, in dismissing Fíthal from the canon of the *speculum*. As Smith notes (1928: 2), the text includes material to be found in the *Tecosca Cormaic*, such as sections 6, 7, 8 and 9 dealing with pleading, behaviour, and human nature. Furthermore, Section 8 of the *SF* is prefaced with a question presumably from Fíthal's son,

Flaithrí, who is not identified in the text (but is identified by Keating, see Comyn and Dinneen 1902-14, vol. 2, 338) according to Smith (1927: 430) in discussing another *Tecosc*.

Smith concludes that the complier of *Tecosca Cormaic* pillaged the *SF* 'for his own purposes' (1928: 2) and put the advice presented directly into the mouth of Cormac, a plagiarism he also unearths in other compilers. But it is equally possible that the charge can be reversed, and that the anthologist of *SF* is the guilty party.

Either way, it does not detract from the argument that *SF* is no more than what Smith had termed 'popular proverbial literature' and, consequently, should find no place in the *speculum* genre. This may prove to be faulty conclusion, perhaps a serious one, but for the moment the content of *Senbríathra Fíthail* is gently left aside as it falls outside the scope of this essay.

Aibidil Luigne maic Éremóin

This particular text, which Smith (who published it as *Aibidil Cuigne maic Emoin*, on which, see Kelly, 1988: 286) assigns to the third century group, is 'but a miscellaneous collection of legal and proverbial maxims which can be traced in many cases to other sources' (Smith 1928a: 45).

In a short but complex sentence, Smith conveys his belief that the name Cuigne mac Emoin is obviously not that of the original author of the sayings, but of the scribe who brought them together from various sources (1928a: 45, but see Kelly, 1988: 286). He offers no reason for distinguishing between the author and scribe or for believing that the original text had been scattered and required subsequent restoration.

The only copy of the text to be found is in the *Yellow Book of Lecan* and was first edited by Meyer; this is the version which Smith further edited and translated (1928a). That the *Alphabet*, as Smith calls it, does not fall into the category of the *speculum*, is immediately evident from his analysis of its content. He argues that it falls into three sections: the first a group of legal maxims; the second a group of *tecosc* passages; and the third a smaller number of proverbial sayings. On inspection, the second section can more accurately be described as proverbial wisdom, being nothing other than a random collection of sayings put down without any discernible structure or stated purpose.

Smith, however, believes that the 'close adherence to formula, the poetic structure, as well as other considerations, make it certain that the *Aibidil* belong to the relatively large number of texts of the *Speculum* or *Fürstenspiegel* type which have come down to us' (1928a: 46). In particular, he holds that the maxim 'enduring is every ruler by whom justice is achieved' (§2.68), closely links the *Aibidil* with the other *Tecosca* texts, a group to which it must have originally belonged. The adage comes nearer to the spirit of the old *Tecosca ríg* than do other texts which bear that name (1928a: 68).

Those comments by Smith give a clue to his definition of a *speculum* as employed here; it is a question of formula, poetic structure and subject matter. The specific characteristic of political advice to a prince is omitted. But since that is the defining purpose of the genre, even according to Smith himself in his 1927 overview, the *Aibidil* cannot be included in the family of wisdom texts whereby an aspiring or new prince is instructed on what to do and what not to do as king.

Notwithstanding some similarities in form and content with the *Tecosca*, the *Aibidil* must be gently placed alongside the *Senbríathra Fíthail* under the heading of work for somebody else. Fortunately, Smith himself had agreed with this: 'Strictly speaking, this text does not belong to the *tecosc* group ... there is no internal evidence that it was the work of a father or tutor for the instruction of his son or lord – in fact, we may safely conclude that it performed no such office' (1927: 431-2). It didn't.

Bríathra Flainn *Fína

The same fate, it has to be confessed, must befall the *Bríathra Flainn *Fína*. This text was first assigned to the seventh and eighth century group by Smith and is generally ascribed to Flann Fína, otherwise known as Aldfrith, King of Northhumbria, who died in 705. Later, Smith re-thought his dating of the text, and assigned it to the third-century group (1927: 433) on the grounds that the form and whole tenor of the text were distinctly of the pagan tradition, and inconsonant with all that was known of the Christian King Aldfrith. The text was edited by Smith in the second half of his 'The *Senbhriathra Fithail* and related texts' (1928: 61–92).

Hull edited a different text also attributed to Flann Fína (1929) shortly after Smith's second thoughts and argued that it was unmistakably religious in tone and spirit, which indeed it is, but also argued that it could not have been written by Flann Fína since the language was Middle Irish (1929: 96–7). Smith vigorously defended himself in his views of the text he edited (1930: 32-3), but the dispute is of little interest here. The *Bríathra Flainn *Fína* no more belongs to the wisdom texts than does a Redemptorist Sermon on the torments of Hell, or the *Vision of Adamnán* for that matter. For a recent edition of the *Bríathra* and a detailed analysis see Ireland (1999).

Three poems

Smith appears to be the only authority including three poems from the seventh–ninth centuries as part of the *speculum* genre. I have not been able to unearth the original texts and can do no more here than briefly summarise Smith's analysis (1927: 434–6).

The first poem (*Díambad messe bad rí réil*), ascribed to Dubh dá Thuath (†783), is of thirty-seven stanzas and is steeped in the pagan tradition, drawing on earlier *tecosca*. The second (*Cert cech ríg co réil*), written by Fothad na Canóine (floruit late eighth–early–ninth century), has a more Christian tone and seems to have been addressed to Áed Oirdnide on his inauguration as king of Tara in ad 815. This would suggest it belongs to the wisdom texts. The third poem in the series (*Ro-cúala, la nech légas libru*) is attributed to St Moling (†696) and found only in the Book of Leinster. It contains 'instructions to a prince' for king Móenach of Munster. In Smith's view, this brief poem of seven stanzas is the earliest of the three and in the content of its closing two verses belongs strictly to the *tecosca* tradition.

Whether these poems should be included among the wisdom texts must await another day. At first sight, their value seems to lie in the hint that the *tecosca* tradition lived on long after the period in which it is thought to have arisen.

Survival of the tradition

The durability of the tradition of wisdom texts is attested by the fact that Smith traces a continuous line from the *Cath Maige Léna* and then *Cath Maige Rath* (in which kings are harangued by their foster fathers on the eve of battle) down to the eighteenth century *Comhairle na bárrsgolóige dá mhac* 'The advice of the wise man to his son'. Indeed, there seems to have been some renewed academic interest among Gaelic scholars in the genre around the turn of the nineteenth century (Smith 1927: 437).

Pride of place goes to Theophilus O'Flanagan who founded the Gaelic Society of Dublin in 1807 and published an English and Latin translation of the inauguration ode, if such it was, of Donnchadh Ó Briain, fourth Earl of Thomond the following year. The ode was composed by Thaddy Mac Brody, or MacBrodin (Tadhg mac Dáire Mhic Bhruaideadha), in the seventeenth century. Smith correctly draws attention to O'Flanagan's doubts as to whether the poem ever formed part of the inauguration ceremony (1927: 436, fn. 2).

O'Flanagan, as his long, erudite and elegant introduction to the poem demonstrates, was an authority on Irish history, folklore and literature who cannot so easily be dismissed from the groves of academe. He exudes that immediate and deep familiarity with this subject that so characterised O'Curry, both of them native speakers steeped in the Gaelic tradition. O'Flanagan is confidently assured in stating that Mac Brody was in conformity 'with the ancient usage of Ireland which entitled the bard to advise his prince' (1808: 27).

He furthermore traces the history of the manuscript with precision and recounts how it came into his possession. Not only does he translate the ode into two languages in verse, he adds copious footnotes explaining the text, such as when Mac Brody makes reference to Feradach and Morann (1808: 39–40), and gives a scholarly, credible explanation for the background to the *Audacht*, which is not found in any modern criticism.

Suffice it to say that the poem faithfully reflects the *tecosca* genre, and commences with those precepts on the role and duties of a king which are so deeply embedded in the Indo-European culture. The concept of the truth manifesting itself in justice leaps out from the ode (lines 149–52, page W45):

> *Daily attend, my prince, thy people's cause,*
> *For this thy duty to dispense the laws,*
> *No easy task, with justice to decide,*
> *The tedious office yet you must abide*

And if he should fail, the terrible consequences are spelled out in familiar detail: war, famine, death, with nature in revolt. The influence of the *Audacht Morainn* and *Tecosca Cormaic* are easily discerned throughout the inauguration ode, even down to the advice of choosing subordinates well: 'to men of violence entrust no power' (line 209, page 48). The poet, in fact, makes specific reference to both texts, while drawing on other apposite historical references back to the earliest times.

Conclusion

The point to be made is that whether the poem was composed in the eleventh or sixteenth century is immaterial to the fact that at the beginning of the nineteenth it was being presented as part of a living tradition, and as being representative of a continuous culture stretching back to the beginning of Irish history. This fact is cause for reflection. It suggests that the *tecosca* may have played a larger role in framing or reflecting political and societal values than the corpus of extant texts suggests.

There are some tantalising hints about other *tecosca* in the literature which, however, do not figure in any of the listings given earlier. If unearthed and analysed they could well add to the corpus of material available and help flesh out the theory. It could also be the case that Bardic poetry contains examples of inauguration odes, per se, which might contain tecosc-like passages or allusions to kingcraft. These are no more than instinctive reactions to both the original texts examined here and the critical literature; they may well prove false. But Mac Brody's poem is hardly an aberration; it seems more like a representative of a class of literature than a historical oddity. It should be taken as a signpost to material for further research.

It would be worthwhile on these grounds to revisit Irish literature from its earliest days down to the famine, to see if other wisdom texts exist. This is a project that should be encouraged, for the cultural rewards would be great. But then, the search for wisdom is its own reward.

Within the strict limits that a *tecosc* text should consist of political advice to a prince, it would seem that only four texts from early Irish literature successfully pass the test. The *Audacht Morainn* and the *Tecosca Cormaic* are consciously intended for that task and are stand-alone as literary compositions. The *Bríatharthecosc Con Culainn* and the *Tecosc Cuscraid* are each essentially part of a larger narrative but, while incidental, are self-contained and appropriate to the task immediately to hand. Despite these differences, the four texts display a thematic unity that goes beyond mere coincidence. Something else is at work – the same mindset, a common cultural instinct, a shared frame of reference, a standard world view.

The ideology which pervades the wisdom texts is grounded in medieval Irish society's view of the cosmic order. That has explained their continued and central emphasis on the sacral role of the king, on the need for him to be the human manifestation of the truth by ensuring that justice is done. But throughout the wisdom texts this fundamental role is not allowed to obscure the reality that it can only properly be fulfilled by one who is endowed with and also cultivates the necessary regal qualities and the political skills to fulfil it properly.

Politics, kingcraft, statesmanship – however this dimension is to be described – is always present. It is this latter feature which gives the texts that particular quality which marks them off from proverbial wisdom or pious sermonising. Having heard what has been said by a wise and trusted mentor, the prince can truly look into the mirror, and see himself as he should be.

Chapter 4

A Window on the Iron Age:

the controversy over the dating of the Ulster Cycle

Summary

This essay reviews Professor Jackson's contention that the Ulster cycle represents a tradition of what once existed and provides us with fragmentary glimpses of Celtic life in the Iron Age.

It begins by placing Professor Jackson's thesis in the context of scholarship at that time, both popular and academic, and demonstrates that his view was broadly consistent with prevailing orthodoxy. Carney is briefly discussed as an exception to the general rule. Jackson's lecture is then analysed, with particular reference to the comparative methodology employed, and it is argued that his conclusions were modestly formulated, prudent and unexceptional.

The cornerstone of more recent scholarship on the Ulster cycle is taken to be best represented by Professor McCone. His book, Pagan past and Christian Present in early Irish literature, is analysed for the counter-argument that the proper frame of reference for the sagas is early Christian Ireland rather than the preceding pagan period. His rejection of the 'nativist' interpretation of the literature and its replacement by a 'biblicist' approach is assessed, and it is argued that the case is convincing, if overstated. Aitchison and his work on the issue is examined because of McCone's use of Aitchison as a key supporting witness.

More recent criticism is reviewed, especially with regard to the archaeological evidence regarding the material culture of the Táin. A brief conclusion argues that the tradition of a tradition lives on in terms of the Ulster cycle offering a glimpse of Iron Age life in Ireland, and that Jackson's window remains of use, even if in need of repair.

Introduction

Professor Jackson's thesis represents what was then (1964), and to some extent still is, an established view on the Ulster cycle. The tales in the cycle were taken as representing a tradition of a society that had existed some four to six centuries before being described in written form. The Ulster cycle was also said to be genuine, in that the tradition had preserved the essential elements of the society in terms of its mores and organisation. Because of this authenticity, the Ulster cycle was regarded, in the modest formulation expressed by Professor Jackson, as a window through which the distant past could be discerned.

Given that the content of the cycle itself was what might nowadays be described as fiction, it was not taken as 'history' in the conventional sense. Unlike Herodotus, Livy or Tacitus, or even Plutarch or Suetonius, who took personalities rather than the broad sweep of historical events as their subject matter, the Ulster cycle was instead regarded as a means whereby the stuff of history could be deduced.

For this thesis to stand it required three supporting premises to be confirmed: first, that the sagas actually reflected the society in which they were situated; second, that they had been transmitted orally across the centuries more or less intact in terms of their essentials; and third, that with the arrival of literacy they had then been committed to writing without significant alteration.

Key to this line of reasoning is the premise that an oral tradition existed; otherwise, the content of the cycle could not have been transmitted down the generations. By definition, such reasoning also demanded that the tradition be inherently conservative, in the literal sense. The other two premises were secondary, in that the sagas could not be basically authentic if they had only been constructed *de novo* with the advent of writing (since they would have been a form of historical fiction as distinct from contemporary fiction) or, if essentially authentic, they could not have been recorded at all unless they had been preserved orally.

What is interesting, by way of a point of departure, is that a tradition had developed about the tradition of the Ulster cycle by the time Ireland's literary history came to be popularised in the late-nineteenth century. For example, Douglas Hyde says that were it not 'thanks to her native annalists, her autochthonous traditions and her bardic histories ... (Ireland) would have fared badly indeed, so far as history goes ... It is towards the middle or close of the fourth century that we come into much closer contact with the Irish, and indeed we know with some certainty a good deal about their internal history, manners, laws, language, and institutions from that time to the present' (1899: 20, 23).

The key phrase here is, of course, 'with some certainty'. That certainty was itself defined by Hyde with a healthy draught of common sense. He added that 'the early Irish writers who redacted the mythical history of the country were no doubt imbued with the spirit of the so-called Greek "logographers" who, when collecting the Greek myths from the poets, desired, while not eliminating the miraculous, yet to smooth away all startling discrepancies and present them in a readable and, as it were, a historical series' (1899: 51).

From this it can be deduced that Hyde believed in the continuity of a tradition, while also accepting that the material had been edited en route so as to conform to the norms of contemporary society. Yet, he perceived a difficulty in this process of accommodating the tradition with the contemporary. Referring to Keating, who wrote a thousand years after the sagas were first composed, Hyde notes that 'from all that we have said it clearly appears that carefully as the Christianised Irish strove to euhemerise their pantheon, they were unable to succeed' (1899: 54).

In other words, he had a sophisticated understanding of the tradition and its rendition in writing – it was at once both representative of its origins in a pagan Ireland and of the Christian Ireland in which it was compiled.

In his foreword to *Gaelic literature surveyed*, Aodh de Blácam makes the same point. Uncannily anticipating the words of Professor Jackson, he claimed that 'in the older portion (of the literature written in Gaelic) is found a window into the early Iron Age, wherein European civilisation was founded' (1930: xiii). De Blácam goes on to argue that 'one of the most remarkable traits of Gaelic literature is that it deals, so as to speak, with a continuous historic present' (*ibid.*). More important, from the viewpoint of this essay, is his claim that 'the same life, the same mode of thought, appears in the eighteenth century as in the eighth' (*ibid.*). This assertion quite evidently confirms what has been styled here as the tradition of a tradition.

In dealing specifically with the tension between paganism and Christianity, de Blácam developed the argument that 'paganism in Ireland rather meant nature unlighted by revelation. It is true that a certain jealousy between pagan scholarship and the Church is traceable during many centuries; but this was the resistance of the natural man to the disciplines of religion. There was little deliberate conflict with the faith ... Certainly Christianity caused no setback to Irish imaginative life: for the great stories ... gain final dramatic point from Christian additions' (1930: 21).

Most critically of all, he added by way of conclusion 'the clergy ... were the transcribers and preservers of the heroic tales' (*ibid.*). It is precisely this conclusion which is, of course, contested by modern scholarship (and constitutes the subject of this essay).

De Blácam's theses are worth repetition as they constituted an integrated framework for analysing the sagas that was generally accepted as standard up to Jackson's time, notwithstanding Carney's critique. De Blácam claims that the older portion of the literature provided a window into the early Iron Age; that a continuity in culture, values and mode of thought had lasted throughout a thousand years of literacy; that there had been a tension between Christianity and paganism but that it had caused no impediment to what he described as 'Irish imaginative life'; that this interplay had heightened the dramatic impact of the sagas; and, finally, that the clergy were the 'transcribers and preservers' of the heroic tales.

He thus marries three points which later scholars regard as logically inconsistent. The sagas are taken as a window on the Iron Age, but simultaneously are regarded as being an amalgam of the pagan and the Christian, while the literati are reduced to mere transcribers and preservers, a classification that seems inherently incompatible with the imaginative act of fusing two separate and, indeed, competing traditions.

Whether this is so is a question addressed later; for the moment it suffices to note that de Blácam is representative of a view that prevailed halfway between the pioneering work of O'Donovan and O'Curry and current scholarship, a period that was itself marked by a resurgence in Celtic studies, notably by German scholars.

Amongst those who helped in the resurgence of interest, not alone in early Irish but modern Irish as well, was Robin Flower, the English scholar forever to be associated with the Blasket Islands. His final publication, *The Irish Tradition* (1947), quite naturally opened with the question of how the written tradition began, and the answer he proposed is, perhaps, the classic of its type.

It consists of eight steps:
- old Irish society was intensely aristocratic. It set great store by memories of past achievement so as to enhance the prestige of the dominant class;
- these memories were kept alive by the poets – that was their function;
- when the mnemonic tradition met the Latin tradition of writing it was fixed in a new form that guaranteed a greater permanence;
- the kings and the poets and the clerics worked together to this end;

- in particular, the men of the new learning set themselves the task from an early stage of identifying how Irish history might be fitted into the scheme of universal history which ruled in the Latin church;
- and the monks worked on this with 'an heroic ardour';
- the language was still Latin;
- but 'it is plain from the entries relating to Irish history that much of the epic material which had come down to us in texts of a later date was already in existence, though exactly in what form it would be hazardous to conjecture' (1947: 4–5).

This last point warrants repetition in view of Flower's reputation and the dissent from Jackson's 'window on the Irish Iron Age' that emerged in more recent times. Flower believed that the earliest Latin compositions give evidence of epic material 'already in existence', i.e. in existence in the Irish language and relating to a society predating the advent of Christianity. From this he deduces that 'by the seventh century the monks had accepted the pagan tradition and put it on one level with the historical material which had come to them under the sanction of the fathers of the Church' (loc. cit.: 5). Because there was no written tradition in Ireland, unlike Israel, Greece and Rome, it was 'desperately necessary to give a validity to the oral tradition upon which they depended for the Irish events in their chronicle' (loc. cit.: 6).

The points of direct interest here are Flower's working assumptions that there was an oral tradition in

Ireland, that it had been accepted by the monkish literati as early as the seventh century and that they were intent on incorporating it into the great schema of world history developed initially by Eusebius.

The motivation for this vast enterprise was, therefore, retrospective, in the sense of being historical; it was also racial rather than religious in that it sought to endow the Irish with a past no less noble or dignified than other ancient civilisations. In short, this was an exercise in racial aggrandisement and is at odds with the later interpretation that its essential purpose was either the religious preoccupations of the literati or the political demands of the then dominant class, or both synthesised into a new integral ideology.

Finally, as this point will emerge again, it is necessary to note that Flower assigned a pivotal role to the *filid* in transmitting the tradition of the past, for 'it was to them that the monastic historians of the sixth and seventh centuries had recourse for all those memories of the past which they desired to put on record in their new medium of writing' (loc. cit.: 4).

At the same time as Flower's final work appeared, Myles Dillon published *Early Irish Literature* (1948), with the express aim of providing an adequate account of early Irish literature; none then existed due to O'Curry and Hull being out of print and the fact that de Blácam dealt with the later period. Dillon sought to present 'the imaginative literature of Ireland in a coherent account' (1948: v).

This coherent account begins by tracing the arrival of the Celts in Ireland and says that they brought with them 'an aristocratic tradition and a highly organised society. The description which Caesar and Polybius have given of Gaulish customs well fits the old Irish world as we know from the sagas' (loc. cit.: xii). This point of correspondence with Jackson is stated with even greater force when Dillon goes on: 'from the heroic sagas ... we get a picture of pre-Christian Ireland which seems genuine' (*ibid.*).

It is not a historical picture, of course, but probably a reflection of the 'social and political conditions of the time which they claim to describe, namely the first century before Christ' (*ibid.*). This phraseology is also strongly reminiscent of Jackson, as will become clear later, although it dates the society of the sagas far earlier than Jackson is prepared to accept and at a point which Aitchison dismisses out of hand. In view of the dispute about the existence of an oral tradition, which is so central to McCone, it is noteworthy that Dillon believes that the sagas have 'evidently a long oral tradition behind them' (*ibid.*). Dillon is, clearly, an exemplar of the tradition.

The resilience of the tradition of a tradition can be attested in a remarkable series of essays, based on the Thomas Davis series of lectures, *Irish Sagas*, with Dillon himself as series editor (Dillon, 1968; henceforth Sagas). All but one of the twelve authorities gathered for this comprehensive review of the sagas take the 'historic present' of Hyde for granted.

In the Introduction to the lectures, Dillon refers to the 'creative memory' at work in the sagas and states that 'the Irish heroic sagas ... preserve, amid much that is pure fantasy, the picture of an old Celtic society such as the ancient historians described as existing in Gaul. Julius Caesar and Strabo and others have described the habits of the Gauls at a feast, their weapons and manner of fighting on the battlefield, and the poetry of their bards. And much of what they tell us is told again in old Irish manuscripts which preserve the Irish sagas, although the sagas are not earlier than the eighth century' (Sagas: 9).

The key phrases here are the description of the sagas as 'the picture of an old Celtic society', despite what is termed 'pure fantasy'. Binchy takes oral tradition for granted when he says that 'the rudiments of the story – *ceithre cnámha an sgéil* – of Fergus mac Léiti go back at least twelve centuries, indeed were probably told in court and camp long before Irish became a written language' (Sagas: 51).

This reference to stories being told in court and camp 'long before' Irish became a written language is all the more striking for the laconic tone in which it is presented; it is simply taken as beyond dispute. Quin, in writing of the oldest version of *Longas Macc nUisnig*, that found in the *Book of Leinster*, says the language points to the eighth or ninth centuries and that some of the verse is undoubtedly older by a century of two. He then adds, tellingly, that 'behind this again we have presumably a period of floating traditions' and, later, that it 'may be survivals of really old tradition' (Sagas: 59).

O'Brien, takes *Fled Bricrenn* as providing 'two very precious survivals linking the Celts of Ireland with those of Western Europe' (Sagas: 78). These are the 'Hero's portion' and the 'Champion's bargain' which he associates with Poseidonius the Stoic, who lived in the last century bc. For O'Brien, this saga, at least, was a window on the world which Poseidonius describes, and which in his own words went back to 'ancient times', i.e. earlier that the first century BC (Sagas: 78).

Nora Chadwick is quite explicit in her belief that an oral tradition was the repository from which the sagas were drawn, like water from a well. She recounts how *Hua Maiglinni* recited ancient deeds of valour prior to the battle of Allen in 722 and uses this fact to claim that 'this standard of memory and of art must have done much to keep alive the history, and the historical conditions of the Heroic Age'.

But, as Hyde and de Blácam had done before her, she is careful to nuance this thesis by adding that 'the nucleus of the ancient traditions has been so well preserved that we are in danger of forgetting that the attitude of the story-teller to his subject, and his artistic methods, gradually changed. At times his own political views colour his presentation of the facts' (Sagas: 80). In short, she quite sensibly introduces political motivations into her analysis, as de Blácam had done with the religious. Nonetheless, she subscribes to the 'window' metaphor when she adds that the accounts of Gaulish feasts in Poseidonius are 'so similar to those of ancient Ireland that some of them could be transferred into an Irish saga without causing the least surprise' (Sagas: 82). For her, *The story of Mac Da Thó's Pig* is 'a glorious travesty of the Ancient World by one who honoured and laughed at its traditions' (Sagas: 89). Here again, there was little doubt about the 'historic present' of the Ancient World;

otherwise it could hardly have been satirised as a sort of ninth century 'Bull Ireland'.

Professor Greene had the *Táin Bó Cúailnge* as his subject matter, the broadest possible canvass of the saga-world. He too thinks that the Ulster cycle, in this case the *Táin*, 'like the rest of the Ulster sagas, preserves pre-Christian traditions' (Sagas: 95), and regards this to be so self-evident that he does not even examine it as a proposition; instead, he asks 'but of what period?' (*Ibid.*). Speculation as to the answer leads him to pose, in terms of the present essay, the most pertinent. Recalling that writing was little known in Ireland before the fifth century, and writing in Irish not much before the seventh, he properly says that 'we have to ask ourselves how long we should allow for an oral tradition which would preserve all these archaic features, free from any admixture of Christian lore' (Sagas: 96).

The answer is brief, to the point and, mercifully, full of common sense: 'Not too long, I would suggest'. He suggests that the stories about the *Ulaid* (Ulstermen) had possibly become part of the stock-in-trade of the literary class just before the coming of Christianity and writing. Admitting that these stories would not have been popular in the 'first flush of missionary learning' he claims that in no country did 'the new learning' make its peace with 'the old learning as quickly or as thoroughly as in Ireland' (Sagas: 97). From this he deduces that the story about the alleged finding of the *Táin* by the poet Seanchán Torpéist in the seventh century was 'just the antiquarians way of saying that it had become respectable to write it down' (*ibid*).

Finally, in line with all of the authorities previously quoted, Greene adheres to the belief that the *Táin* was not just written down but rearranged as well, and he agrees that there is probably a good deal of truth in Thurneysen's suggestion that 'the *Táin* in its present form has been influenced by the Aeneid; the writers were out to provide Ireland with a national epic' (Sagas: 98).

This formulation of the *Táin* subscribes to the general theory that the content is an admixture of the archaic and the then contemporary and was the product of a cultural truce between the old and the new learning, perhaps more properly described as the dynamic fusion of imaginative elements to create a new cultural compound. But, the twist in the plot is that, for Greene, the purpose of this reaction is to compose 'a national epic' similar to that of a pagan Rome, which had, of course, been based in turn on those of pagan Greece. This is a long way from adapting archaic material for purposes of Christian proselytising; in fact, it is the opposite. As such, it corroborates Jackson's use of the Iliad as an analogy for the Ulster cycle, as he does in the early part of his lecture, 'The oldest Irish tradition: A window on the Iron Age' 1964: 2–8).

Yet, for all that, Greene analyses a passage relating to Cú Chulainn's boyhood and, while stating that it could hardly have been written much before the ninth century, says 'but there is no admixture at all of the classical or ecclesiastical elements' (Sagas: 102). In short, the story is one example of what some might describe as an archaic residue to be found in the *Táin*, but which others regard as its very essence.

O'Daly is less personal in her treatment of *Togail Bruidne Da Derga* and quotes Lucius Gwynn and O'Rahilly as authorities for the argument that the story is part of a 'tradition of a sudden overthrow of an ancient order of things' (Sagas: 106), which could go as far back as the third century bc.

Gerard Murphy, in treating *Acallam na Senórach*, contrasts the literary traditions of Finn mac Cumaill and his fían with that of Cú Chulainn and the Ulidian heroes of the heroic tradition; the first was a more recent innovation, the other was 'firmly fixed by age-old literary custom' (Sagas: 121). For Breathnach, *Tóraigheacht Dhiarmada agus Gráinne* 'is a theme that has come out of the deep well of immemorial time in which Myth has its source ... it is an elaboration of a half-forgotten, half-remembered thought from the treasure-trove of the Gaelic race's timeless memory' (Sagas: 147).

Carney deals with *Cath Maige Muccrime*, a story of the origins of the greatest dynastic kindred that Ireland has known, and is primarily concerned with the power of the underlying myth down to the early twentieth century. His references to earlier traditions are necessarily oblique but, even so, fit into the framework presented by the other contributors. He refers, for example, to 'the remote origins of the contemporary ruling kindred' from which the author of the saga shaped the myth and deduces that 'for certain details' he had drawn upon 'two pre-existing traditions' (Sagas: 152–3).

The theme of the essay is, itself, a powerful if unwitting corroboration of the endurance of tradition across the centuries to the point that it still 'has such potency, is so endemic to the soil that it could inspire its recreation in our own time' (Sagas: 148).

In the final essay from the Thomas Davis series of lectures, on *Fingal Rónáin*, Greene argues that 'the idea of pure literature, the story for the story's sake, had developed in the three centuries or so since the old oral tradition came to terms with the new Latin learning.' This 'old oral tradition' contained 'very old material' which, in the case of this particular story, had a trace of an archaism in that it is 'completely pagan both in spirit and expression' (Sagas: 162–3).

Without forcing the thesis too far, it can be said that all but one of the lecturers in the series subscribe in some form to the proposition that prior to Christianity an old oral tradition had existed, had then come into contact with the Latin learning, had been transformed and enriched in the process but, nonetheless, had retained elements of archaism that were completely pagan despite being written down by monastic scribes.

Dillon, in analysing the narrative form of the sagas, comprising prose and poetry, concludes that it is the ancient Indo-European form which, in Ireland, 'survived down to the Middle Ages, illustrating what can be shown in various other ways, the great archaism of Irish tradition' (Sagas: 13).

It was just prior to this Thomas Davis series of lectures that Professor Jackson delivered his Rede Lecture in 1964. As will be seen, his general approach to the Ulster cycle conforms to that of the ten Irish authorities assembled for the purpose of giving a definitive account of the Irish sagas in the light of contemporary scholarship. That it was to be a definitive account is beyond dispute, for the Thomas Davis lectures were intended 'to provide a popular form of what is best in Irish scholarship and the sciences' (Sagas: 5).

The lectures, taken individually and collectively, and the general introduction by Dillon as the series editor, thus represent the prevailing view of Irish scholarship on the sagas at its most authoritative and provide an appropriate context in which Jackson's contemporaneous analysis can best be assessed.

One caveat, at least, is necessary and needs repetition. As previously indicated, the team of scholars assembled by Dillon included Professor James Carney, whose *Studies in Irish Literature and Hstory* (1955) had already introduced a line of reasoning which pitted the 'nativist' interpretation of the sagas against what had come to be known as the 'biblicist'.

His proposition was that 'there is no Irish saga extant which does not show some sign, however slight, of what nativists would call "monkish redaction"' (1955: 305). He elaborated the point by arguing that 'since literary redaction is an apparent and incontrovertible fact (the sagas are, after all, written) we are not justified in assuming that the "monkish additions" are limited to those cases where they are immediately and accidentally obvious' (306).

His general thesis about the form and provenence of the sagas was expressed with force and simplicity as follows: 'My contention here is that, as in the case of verse, the form and technique of Irish prose sagas have a double line of descent: one line is that of pre-literate oral narration, the other (and perhaps in the case of the better-known sagas, the predominant line) derives from the mixed Christian classical culture of the earliest monastic period' (*ibid.*).

Carney therefore identifies three influences at work: the Irish oral tradition, classical literature and Christianity. In respect of the classical influences he had no doubt 'but that Homer ... is the ultimate ancestor' of such scenes in early Irish literature (313). As for the oral tradition, 'without any doubt this [early Irish saga] literature was based in part upon an oral tradition going back to the remote pre-Christian past.

But the traditional element is often a mere nucleus because the Christian authors, in presenting the pre-Christian past, drew not only on native material but on their total literary experience' (321). Carney in later life tempered this analysis somewhat but, nevertheless, his argument rounds off what was the conventional wisdom of the time in which Jackson delivered his lecture.

Jackson's central argument is that the Ulster cycle, although 'historically bogus' (1964: 44) and superimposed with 'a thick layer of biblical and antiquarian ecclesiastical learning' (46), nonetheless 'provide[s] us with a picture – very dim and fragmentary, no doubt, but still a picture – of Ireland in the Early Iron Age' (5). Jackson sets himself the task of proving that the Ulster cycle provided a window on the Early Iron Age by first sketching out the contours of the picture itself (dim and fragmentary as he describes it) and then attempting to date it.

This seems an unexceptional mission in the light of the then contemporary scholarship, and even more so of the context in which the lecture was given. It was intended for those scholars interested in the early history of the British Isles who, for reasons of their professional interests or specialities, were less aware than they should be of 'this extraordinary archaic fragment of European literature' (1964: 5), and he modestly claimed to be presenting nothing new in the hypothesis that the sagas 'belong in fact to a "pre-historic" Ireland' (4).

The lecture, was, as it were, no more than a primer, an introduction to a relatively unknown subject or, if one wishes, a condensed popularisation of Irish literature, in this case the Ulster cycle, following in the steps of Hyde, de Blácam and others.

Jackson's methodology in arriving at a picture of the society inherent in the Ulster cycle is to compare it with Gaulish and British society prior to their destruction by Rome. A range of classical authors is adduced: Caesar, Diodorus Siculus, Strabo, Athenaeus and, of course, Poseidonius (whose lost history served as the primary source for the others), with Aristotle, Polybius, Livy and Ammanius Marcellinus cited for corroborative detail.

Their descriptions of the way of life of the Gauls, and to some extent of the Britons, in the Early Iron Age are then summarised and compared for parallels with those portrayed in the Ulster cycle. These include (1964: 28–43):

- social organisation
- dress
- diet
- feasting
- clientship

- weaponry
- military mores (head-hunting, the champion's portion)
- superstitions
- functional roles (baird, *filid* and druid)
- religious beliefs
- social behaviour and
- group psychology

Based on this comparison, Jackson argues for a 'general agreement between the habits of the Gauls and Britons in the first century bc and those of the early Irish' (1964: 43). Having established a broad correspondence between the three societies, Gaulish, British and Irish, he examines the evidence for dating the Ulster cycle on the basis of the following line of reasoning.

The *La Tène* culture came to Ulster from Gaul via northern Britain in the second century bc, or earlier; the immigrant people retained their identity for some centuries; it follows that the formation of the tradition on which the cycle is based falls between the second century bc and the fourth century ad, as the *Ulaid* kingdom was broken into pieces in the fifth century; the people of the cycle were pagans and the cycle contains no traces of Christianity; the first recension of the *Táin* is known to have existed already in the first half of the eighth century and may have been in writing as early as the middle of the seventh; the stories had been handed on previously by oral tradition, probably for about 300 years (loc. cit.: 43–55). Surprisingly, Jackson does not put an approximate date or period on the Ulster society of the sagas but, rather, opts for a broader less contentious conclusion that the stories were put together in, say, the fourth century ad, and not earlier.

The two tasks having been completed, Jackson ends by claiming that the account of the life and civilisation depicted in the Ulster cycle (55) is demonstrably older than the fifth century; is extraordinarily similar to that of the Gauls and Britons in the couple of centuries before they were absorbed by Rome; and the reason for this is that the Gauls, Britons and Irish were all living in cultures which were local expressions of a Celtic Iron Age whose common roots lay in Gaul in the third century BC.

Jackson accordingly submits that it is 'not altogether fanciful or without justification' to say that if we want to know what it was to be a late *La Tène* Celt and what life in the Early Iron Age was like then we can get 'some notion' of it by reading the Ulster cycle (55).

This extraordinarily modest formulation rests, of course, on the proposition that an oral tradition existed and it is central to both the picture of the society as conveyed in the cycle and to its dating as about 300 years before first being written down. It does, however, accept that Christian and classical influences were at work and that the content had consequently been modified, altered or nuanced, as had the genealogies (45), although this aspect of the matter is not examined in any detail, being outside the scope of the lecture and the purpose for which it was intended.

Taken on its own merits, and within the context in which it was delivered, the central thrust of the lecture is broadly consistent with the scholarship of the day and makes no claims other than those which could be corroborated by other scholars or disciplines, notably archaeology and classical literature.

The strength of Jackson's argument (but also its potential vulnerability) lies in the comparative methodology employed. If the classical authors are to be taken as credible authorities, then the life and habits of the ancient Gauls and Britons are indeed the yardstick by which the life and habits of the *Ulaid* are to be assessed and, on the basis of the parallels identified, it is surely reasonable to conclude that a striking similarity exists.

Furthermore, if that culture or civilisation existed as far back as the first century bc in Gaul and Britain, then it is not unreasonable to assume that it existed too in the Ulster of the sagas at some point either then or later. Jackson opts for a much later period because of his caution regarding the durability of an oral tradition; rather than pushing the date of the sagas back to the traditional time of Christ he urges prudence and, by implication, settles for sometime between the first and second century AD.

While this is commendable in terms of scholarship, it raises an intriguing question not discussed by Jackson: if his own dating of the cycle is accepted, what is one to say of the fact that the *La Tène* culture in Ulster continued unchanged, at least in the essentials identified by him, for some centuries after the classical authors had described it?

And what does that tell us of its tenacity in preserving itself, of the means by which it achieved cultural continuity and of the manner in which it would react to an external shock, such as the arrival of Christianity?

One historian offers a view on the durability of tradition, which not only highlights the prudential approach of Jackson but also provides some answers to these questions. Hughes wrote the introduction to Otway-Ruthven's *A History of Medieval Ireland* (Hughes: 1968) in which she claims that it was 'the learned class who guarded the traditions of a people ... they maintained a continuous tradition intact from the pre-Christian past' up to the point of the Norman conquest (11).

Indeed, on the first page of the introduction she puts Jackson in the shade by asserting that 'Irish civilisation in the tenth century probably still had much in common with that of the Gaulish Celts before the Romans arrived'. What, or how much, was in common is not made clear but she has no doubt that 'the heroic tales of the Ulster cycle ... provide a self-consistent and circumstantial account of a pre-Christian society which seems to be similar to that which Roman occupation destroyed in Gaul and Britain' (3). She agrees, therefore, with Jackson that the tales 'provide vivid pictures of pre-Christian Irish society' and is sympathetic to his arguments as to their dating. On the impact of Christianity she tends towards the Jackson position by asserting that the monastic schools were in the main 'sympathetic to secular learning' and as a result 'Christianity gave to secular learning another medium, the written record, and at the same time enriched the intellectual life of Ireland with a new literature and new ideas' (1968: 23-4). Despite this, she persists in describing Irish civilisation up to the Normans as archaic, with its roots bedded deep in a pre-Christian past.

This view of Irish society stretching from the era of the sagas to that in which they were recorded in extant literature (in fact, a millennium, give or take a few hundred years) is contested by what has come to be known as the Biblicist School, of which McCone is the most trenchant representative. In the Prologue to his *Pagan Past and Christian Present in Early Irish Literature* (1990), he assembles his cast and marshals his arguments against 'nativist' orthodoxy.

The fundamental argument is that 'most extant early Irish sagas bore a clear and deep monastic imprint, whatever their remote origins in pagan oral tradition' (ix). The authority for this is Carney, following in the footsteps of Thurneysen. The next step is to elaborate on the nature of the 'monastic imprint', and for this purpose the authority is Ó Corráin who has assembled evidence, in McCone's words, of 'monastic propagandists and genealogists' acting as 'ruthless reshapers of the past in the interests of the present' (1990: ix).

This Orwellian representation of medieval Ireland is reinforced by invoking a third authority, Ó Cathasaigh, who is said to have shown that the early Irish sagas are 'deliberate literary compositions primarily geared to contemporary concerns rather than antiquarian assemblages, however archaic or traditional the elements so manipulated' (*ibid.*). And, in a coup de grace, Ó Corráin and Breatnach are cited as authorities for the re-evaluation of the early Irish secular law tracts, 'the most jealously guarded of all traditionalist bastions', and are said to have made 'an incontrovertible case for monastic authorship' (*ibid.*).

When these pieces of the jigsaw are fitted together an altogether different picture of medieval Ireland becomes visible than that displayed in the 'nativist' gallery under the curatorship of Dillon in the Thomas Davis lecture series. Early Christian Ireland is transformed from an 'abnormal and stagnant' sideshow into a major production set in 'an early medieval European civilisation'.

McCone is certain that this alternative picture of early medieval Ireland amounts to a 'revolution in scholarly attitudes', which successfully marries archaism on the one hand and a contemporary modernism on the other. He offers a provisional synthesis and overview of this revolutionary approach by arguing that despite the diversity of early Irish literature, it is rooted in a 'coherent, far-reaching and flexible construct' forged by 'monastic men of letters' whose 'level of scholarship, intellectual analysis and imagination', when brought to bear upon this 'gargantuan undertaking', blossomed into a dynamic, creative, erudite and cohesive monastically based civilisation from the sixth century ad onwards which, *inter alia*, 'helped to lead Britain and Europe out of the Dark Ages' (1990: ix–x).

This panoramic view of medieval Ireland is not novel, indeed it has a well-established ancestry going back to the 'island of saints and scholars', through Keating, then via O'Curry and later populariser, like Hyde and de Blácam, down to such present-day exponents as Cahill with his *How The Irish Saved Civilisation* (Cahill, 1995).

But what is novel in the McCone thesis is the breadth of erudition, the extent of the scholarship, the wealth of references, the scale of ambition and, more particularly, the sustained momentum of the synthesis, which fuses minute detail with broad sweeping conceptual insights. All in all, it is a formidable achievement worthy of what is a revolution in scholarly, as distinct from popular, attitudes.

At its core, the synthesis produced by McCone displaces the nativist orthodoxy of the monastic scribes as tame transcribers of received tradition with the diametrically different role of ruthless reshapers of the past for the political purposes of the present.

Instead of being windows on the past, the sagas are a snapshot of the times in which they were composed. They tell us more about the Ireland of the day than a distant past or, if that is pushing the point too far, as much about the world of the monastic scholars as that of the Ulster cycle.

Their essential purpose is propaganda, not history; the aim of the literati is not to conserve pagan traditions intact but to modify and adapt them and thereby establish a new Christian tradition.

This reshaping of the sagas is but part of a larger enterprise embracing the genealogies and the law tracts, an enterprise which itself is a reflection of a vibrant, creative, outward looking civilisation and the product of a new culture born by merging the Celtic with the Christian and the classical.

For the synthesis to hold it must disprove the existing orthodoxy, a task which McCone attempts without undue preliminaries. By the second page of his book, for example, he names its high priests (Dillon, Binchy, Jackson, MacCana and Ó Coileáin) and lays bare their broad common standpoint on what he describes as the 'most influential and fashionable approach to the evaluation of early Irish literature'. The main elements of this approach are identified as a tradition which is:

- conservative
- transmitted orally, in the main
- continuous with a pagan past, and
- rooted in Celtic and Indo-European antiquity.

The two major props of this approach are said to be the Indo-European hypothesis and theories about oral transmission. The nativists also minimised the role of Christianity and literacy in terms of their impact on the secular genres of the literature. These props are to be kicked aside so that the whole 'nativist' edifice comes tumbling down.

But, equally importantly, the minimisation of the role of Christianity and literacy is to be corrected by maximising their separate but interdependent, or complementary, functions as the reshapers of the literature.

These, then, are the three broad tasks upon which McCone embarks with commendable vigour and an awesome energy. But the temptation inherent in these tasks is that the ambition to modify the Indo-European hypothesis and recast the theory of the oral tradition may be taken to the point of negating them altogether; the temptation is almost irresistible if the complementary ambition is to maximise the role of the ruthless reshapers, for what is left by way of a credible explanation of early Irish literature if the two props of nativist orthodoxy are brought crashing down? Nothing much, it could be said, other than the role of the clerical literati. It is a temptation that McCone does not altogether resist.

It is extraordinarily difficult to summarise the full sweep of McCone's analysis, for it rages on like a torrent for over 250 pages. But one attempt to encapsulate the logic and content of the argumentation might go like this. The Indo-European hypothesis is first questioned, and one is warned to 'beware of facile assumptions with the Dumézilian system', which had previously been subject to criticism (1990: 3). No more is heard of it from that point onwards (or so the index would suggest). Then, the attractions of orality to nativist scholars are shown to be misplaced because 'recent anthropological studies of oral traditions have tended to stress the decisive role of contemporary social and political factors in shaping them' (*ibid.*: 4).

In short, the process of transmission influences a non-literate society's view of the past. Myth and history merge into one, and elements of the cultural heritage which cease to have a contemporary relevance are discarded, forgotten or transformed.

Consequently, oral traditions are conditioned by the society in which they flourish and, rather than being in stasis, tradition is in a state of flux; in fact, it is not tradition as conventionally understood, but a soon to be forgotten or reshaped version of the past which exists only at a given point in time.

It follows logically that there is no way of tracing change back across the generations since, by definition, there is no verifiable documentary record of the past.

There is no continuous past, only an ever-shifting present. By way of evidence for this thesis, the findings of Goody and Vansina are quoted (*ibid.*).

This is a stark view of the ultimate meaninglessness of an oral tradition, perhaps too harsh. Nevertheless, Nagy and Slokia are cited to corroborate the argument that pre-Christian Celtic literature was not preserved meaninglessly by the scribes, but rather was appreciated by an audience which understood it 'at some level other than pre-Christian myth', although, prima facie, this does not quite substantiate the conclusions of Goody and Vansina.

Indeed, Nagy in the introduction to his major work, *Conversing with Angels and Ancients* (1996), asserts that the literary project of the literati 'resonated with the performative traditions of poetic composition and story-telling that predated the coming of Christianity to Ireland' (1996).

He weakens his credibility as a witness for the prosecution, however, when he immediately goes on to claim that 'these traditions continued to play a vital role in Irish cultural life throughout the medieval period, arguably outliving the literary tradition itself' (*ibid.*).

His focus is different to that of McCone; it is what he calls an innovation in the history of western Christianity. His thesis is specific: the Irish saint mediated not only on a religious but also on a literary plane. The *noíb* could rehabilitate and sponsor the recording of a pre-Christian 'native' past discredited in the eyes of a Christian present, sanction the literary preservation of some of the elements of that past, and discover the past anew for a present that had lost touch with its roots (1996: xiii).

This thesis is hardly in tune with that developed by McCone, not least when it is applied to the *Táin*, for example. In that case, the role of the saints was 'the untrammelled transmission of the past remembered ... working together harmoniously towards the restitution of the past in a modern, written form. Everyone and everything, including past and present, prove ultimately compatible, and so the prize, the *Táin* is won complete' (1996: 311).

The restitution of the past, as he described it, does not quite gel with McCone's concept of the past ruthlessly reshaped. In fact, it could be described as the inverse.

Aitchison is, however, quoted by McCone as a substantive rebuttal of Jackson. Aitchison's use of the new approach to oral tradition leads him to conclude that the Ulster cycle tales are 'neither the literary transcriptions of Iron Age oral traditions, nor do they offer a "window" on Iron Age society' (Aitchison, 1987: 87). Nothing could be more definitive than that.

Far from being a window on the past, the Ulster cycle is a remarkable potential addition to 'our knowledge of secular and religious affairs in northeastern Ireland during the second half of the first millennium AD' (*ibid.*). And this conclusion by Aitchison, which is central to McCone's construct, is used by him to devastating effect: 'It can now be regarded as axiomatic that, assumed oral origins for some of its constituents notwithstanding, the proper frame of reference for early Irish literature is early Christian Ireland rather than the preceding pagan period' (McCone 1990: 4).

This short sentence is so loaded that it demands careful analysis in order to disentangle its various components and subject them to scrutiny. First of all, Aitchison is taken as having established an axiom, i.e. a self-evident truth. Second, the role of oral tradition is admitted, although heavily qualified by being cast as partial and problematic. Third, the frame of reference for early Irish literature is early Christian Ireland, whereas Aitchison is quite explicit in confining the relevance of the Ulster cycle to its proper geographical location of northeastern Ireland (1987: 105-11). McCone has, as it were, applied Aitchison's conclusion to the whole of Ireland. While this reasoning is logically defensible, being entirely consistent with Aitchison's analysis, it nonetheless, exposes McCone's enthusiasm for universalising from the particular; temptation is at work.

Where does all this leave Jackson? By this early stage of the synthesis he has already been disposed of by McCone in summary fashion. He is the author of a 'small but influential book' (McCone, 1990: 3): it was, of course, a lecture. According to McCone, Jackson is the representative of the Homeric approach to early Irish literature, which emphasises its 'formulaic oral composition and transmission' and ascribes a 'secondary and essentially uncreative later role of writing' in its survival. He is a believer in the ability of a 'strictly regulated oral tradition to preserve a reasonably accurate, if patchy, record of earlier social and political conditions over a long period' (1990: 3).

But this representation of Jackson, fair and accurate as it may be, is not subject to critical analysis on its own terms but is simply taken as a prototype of the school which believes that the picture of the past was 'preserved orally until it entered an apparently equally reactionary written record' (4). This prototype is then engulfed by the scholarly criticism quoted above.

The central pre-occupation of McCone is to remind us that we have no direct knowledge of a presumed oral tradition (as discussed earlier), and that what have come down to us from the early Christian period are exclusively the written products of the monastically educated (a broader term than 'monastic men of letters', those ruthless reshapers of the past quoted in the *Prologue to Pagan past and Christian Present in Early Irish literature* (1990). The key point for McCone is that the 'nativist' school puts the cart before the horse in according primacy to the unattested oral tradition and its pagan origins, rather than to clerical and monastic literacy (1990: 5).

In order to establish this point, and thereby close the window on the past so that it emits only a chink of light, McCone is at pains to disprove MacCana's thesis that the monastic literati were 'remarkably liberal and sympathetic to pagan tradition' and, most important of all, that had it not been 'for their goodwill and enthusiasm it would have gone the way of most oral tradition in a changing and literate world' (6).

MacCana had accepted that there was censorship in the monastic recording of native tradition, but this does not save him from McCone, who dispatches the former's 'benign ecumenism' model by invoking O'Rahilly. This is only to be expected, but O'Rahilly is a difficult witness. For example, he made the following observations, which would have weakened the McCone argument: 'For the pre-Christian period contemporary record fails us; but fortunately we are not left completely in the dark. In early Christian Ireland the popular memory was extraordinarily tenacious and conservative regarding the various origins of the different strata of the population; and with the help of these popular traditions, which have in part been preserved, it is possible to trace our history, in some of its broad outlines, back to a period antecedent to the Christian era' (O'Rahilly 1946: 263). O'Rahilly was here writing about history, such as the *Lebor Gabála* and the genealogies, as well as the sagas, under a chapter headed 'History or Fable?' (260–85).

His view, as expressed above, seems closer to that of Hughes and MacCana than to that of McCone. Analysing the Ulidian Tales in that chapter he answers the question posed in the chapter's title by stating that they are 'wholly mythical in origin and they have not the faintest connection with anything that could be called history' (271).

Despite this analysis, he does state in the Preface of his book that, after criticism has done its legitimate utmost regarding the history of pre-Christian Ireland, 'there remains a modest residuum from which important historical deductions can be drawn'. For that purpose, he claims that for a critical examination of early Irish traditions a 'thorough knowledge of pagan beliefs and myths' is indispensable and makes it possible to 'unravel the origins of the Ulidian and other early Irish sagas' (O'Rahilly 1946: vi).

On these grounds he is a somewhat unsatisfactory witness for the case against MacCana, although McCone saves the day by remarking that the presence of supernatural beings and features in the sagas only proves that the 'early Irish clerks are scarcely more convincing as totalitarians than as liberals' (1990: 7).

This conundrum is resolved by McCone in two lengthy chapters. Having previously examined recent trends in the scholarly study of Norse sagas, which conform with, or confirm, the biblicist theory (19), and having established that early Christian Ireland had a 'reasonably typical medieval western European social structure in which Church and state were inextricably linked' (24), McCone solves the riddle by first admitting that originally pagan elements found their way into 'a creative interplay of native and biblical models' of literature but were certainly not 'part of a deliberate policy to preserve manifestations of a paganism detested by the church and her associates' (34).

On the basis of various studies in the 'vast corpus' of early Irish literature, he argues convincingly that the examples quoted should give us 'some idea of the enormous technical and stylistic variety and sophistication of early Irish narrative literature' (52) and that, in the words of Carney, the traditional element is often 'a mere nucleus because the Christian authors, in presenting a pre-Christian past, drew not only on native material but upon their total literary experience' (Carney 1955: 321).

This formulation is somewhat harder than those expressed elsewhere by Carney, as has been noted earlier. For example, at one stage Carney says that 'every early saga is complex, containing elements which derive in varying proportions from native oral tradition and from the contemporary literate culture of early Ireland (1955: 278), and again, 'the early Irish author, even when dealing with the remote pagan past ... shows signs of being influenced by the early Christian culture of Ireland' (279).

The choice of quotation by McCone from Carney is, perhaps, another example of over-enthusiasm in making a case which by this stage in the development of his thesis is already well-established. It seems somewhat overdone to talk of 'backward-looking isolationism of the post-war nativist school' (1990: 53).

The technical and stylistic variety and sophistication of the sagas thus knocks over the second prop of the nativist school and opens the way for the final part of the answer to the conundrum of the liberalism and totalitarianism of the literati. They had produced a 'thoroughly integrated hybrid medium in which all extant early Irish literature, history and mythology can be rooted ... the matrix continued to be able to adapt and absorb elements from the Bible or elsewhere as the occasion demanded' (McCone 1990: 79).

To quote some examples: *Scéla Muicce Meic Da Thó* is a 'deadly earnest, if at times amusing, moral satire ... geared by its monastic author to Christian principles' (77); *Immram Brain* and *Echtrae Chonlai* are thoroughly Christian allegories (80) and, specifically, the tale of Conlae is 'an allegory of the global and individual conflict between pagan iniquity and Christian virtue ... the claims of this world and those of everlasting life' (82).

Accordingly, it transpires that 'mythological, historicising, allegoristic and typological factors could be combined freely and often inextricably together by the early Christian Irish literati to modify pre-existing narratives and generate new ones' (82).

Hence, it follows, that many of the sagas are not the passive transcriptions of a liberal, accommodating, sympathetic monastic class, as with MacCana, but new sagas consciously composed as part of overall control of the *senchus*. To what end? To enable the church and her allies to 'monitor and modulate the values and institutions of the governing class as a whole' while, of course, allowing scope for various political groups to press their own claims (82). And how was this achieved? By allowing native mythological modes of thought and expression to 'resonate happily' with those of the Bible (82).

The upshot was an ideological framework, which bound church and state together and was 'thoroughly in tune with the various spiritual and secular interests of a monastically oriented learned class' (82-3). Clearly, this formulation puts the interests of the monastic class in pride of place and suggests that, whatever reservations may be entertained as to the efficiency of monastic censorship, it had established a form of thought-control not seen again until the Ireland of 1922-90.

Presumably, it was this achievement which allows McCone to argue that, for all its peculiarities, medieval Ireland was typical of contemporary society in Western Europe and hence, played a role in its shaping that is as credible now as it was relevant then.

As stated earlier, McCone arrived at these conclusions by taking it as axiomatic that the proper frame of reference for early Irish literature is early Christian Ireland (1990: 4). This set conventional wisdom on its head, as scholars and popularisers had been virtually unanimous in believing that the frame of reference was the preceding pagan period.

Aitchison's role in establishing the axiom is so central that his analysis of the Ulster cycle demands separate detailed scrutiny to see if, indeed, he reduces Jackson's elegant edifice to mere academic rubble. In this task it is helpful to recall that Aitchison was a post-graduate student in archaeology at the time of writing his 'The Ulster Cycle: heroic image and historical reality' (1987) and that, not unnaturally, his ultimate pre-occupation was that archaeologists (and historians) should not take the Ulster cycle as a 'source of data from which odd excerpts concerning early Irish society or material culture may be extracted' (1987: 13).

The motivation for this viewpoint related to the role archaeologists had assumed in regard to Celtic scholarship, as exemplified by Jackson. That role was one of subservience to a thesis established outside their own discipline; they had become validators of Jackson and, so, had abandoned their objectivity and impartiality. That seems a fair representation of Aitchison's criticism of his profession for the following reasons. Having described Jackson's treatment of the epic literature as representing the debasement of its contents, Aitchison complains that archaeologists turned to these sources 'in order to give a more vivid, detailed and accurate impression of the nature of Celtic Iron Age society than they believed the archaeological record alone could ever provide' (*ibid.*).

Whether or not this damning indictment is true remains a matter for archaeologists, but it indicates that Aitchison was a man with a mission intent on restoring the integrity of archaeological scholarship. This mind-set needs to be taken into account when evaluating his arguments, especially as it is only exposed at the very end of his article, although, in fairness, he hints at this in his opening when he says that the episodes of the Ulster cycle, and the *Táin* in particular, 'have exercised a profound influence on archaeologists' perception of early Irish society' (88). More particularly, for the purposes of this essay, this background serves as a filter for assessing his criticisms of Jackson. He wishes to liberate archaeology and, to do so, coins his own version of a liberation theology.

Such commendable zeal has, however, its own pitfalls: it may lead to an unfair, even untenable, representation of the scholarly arguments to be rebutted. Aitchison seems open to that charge in, at least, the following respects. First, it is essential for Aitchison to establish that Jackson implied there was 'a distinct break between the pagan and Christian periods', as the explicit paganism of the literature would then establish it had been composed 'before about mid-fifth century' (1987: 90). But the source quoted from Jackson (1964: 24) contains no such implication. Next, while he properly asserts that Jackson drew parallels between Gaulish and Irish society from the works of Roman writers, Aitchison then adds 'mainly Caesar' (1987: 91). This qualification is biased and misrepresents Jackson's use of the classical authorities (see above). More importantly, Aitchison claims that Jackson (1964: 50) states the archaic culture of the epic literature had 'survived unaltered in Ireland until the advent of Christianity' (1987: 92), whereas Jackson's own words are 'lingered on' (1964: 50), a much more nuanced statement in line with his overall tenet.

Finally, he accuses Jackson of gross inconsistency in using the 'historical-geographic' school of literacy and linguistic study in his approach to the Ulster cycle, and says that this approach is 'essentially no different from that adopted by Ridgeway almost sixty years earlier' in a paper of which he says Jackson is 'highly critical' (1987: 93).

On examination, Jackson is seen to be far less categorical, in that he says 'Ridgeway had the right idea, but unfortunately spoiled it all by a slip in his reasoning' (1964: 49), and then corrects this slip in reasoning by amending the date of the cycle from the birth of Christ to the more imprecise and open-ended 'before the fifth century' (1964: 50). This hardly seems like high criticism and, at the very least, exonerates Jackson from the charge of methodological inconsistency. On the contrary, these examples from Aitchison's use of Jackson demonstrate that Aitchison was too eager to put words in his mouth, so that Jackson could be more easily refuted and ultimately demolished.

Despite these enthusiasms, Aitchison nonetheless offers a well-rounded, tightly knit set of arguments in his critique of Jackson. They fall under seven broad headings; mythology, religious beliefs, society, its social and historical context, early Irish history and archaeology. These are synthesised into the conclusion that the 'early epic literature does not constitute a legitimate source for the study of pagan Celtic society, a "window on the Iron Age"'. Hence, the nature of that social system cannot be discerned, nor can it be confirmed by archaeology (1987: 113). Taking the headings individually in the sequence adopted will help in the ultimate assessment of the conclusion.

First, in respect of mythology, Aitchison charges Jackson with underestimating the mythological content of the tales, so that he can strengthen their 'basis in reality' and so provide a 'reliable impression' of the society in which they are situated. In contrast, mythology 'pervades the very fabric of the tales', a prime example of which is the plot of the *Táin* (89) and, because of this, a distinction cannot be made between the realistic and the fantastic (90). This is a statement of opinion, which seems to be unsubstantiated by a reading of Jackson.

On the matter of religious beliefs, Aitchison simply charges Jackson with the belief that the Ulster cycle is devoid of any reference to Christianity and hence was composed in a pagan society. This, of course, has implications for dating its composition, especially as Jackson is further charged with implying a distinct break between the pagan and Christian periods (90). As indicated above, this latter allegation cannot be substantiated. The society argument is, perhaps, more fundamental as it challenges, or rebuts as Aitchison would see it, the use of classical authorities in establishing similarities between Gaulish and Irish society. Their 'geographical and historical specificity' (91) is adduced (by reference to one study on Poseidonius) and so cannot be employed uncritically 'to form a generalised account of second and first century bc Gaulish society', and certainly not Caesar whose account is 'superficial and ethnocentric' (91).

On the other hand, social customs, like the champion's portion, are universalised by Aitchison as 'what might be expected among members of a warrior aristocracy within almost any barbarian society' (91), in order to deny their specificity in the context of the Ulster cycle. Aitchison is having his own champion's portion here, and eating it. Decapitation similarly gets short shrift, as it was 'also practiced in early historic Ireland'; and the use of the chariot is similarly dismissed as evidence for dating (91-2). This is a substantial point, as will be seen later from Mallory (1992a: 147-51).

The upshot is that Aitchison can claim that in respect of social structure, ritual practices and material culture, Jackson's argument can be contradicted 'in each case by the culturally and historically specific contexts of the sources which he employs, and by evidence of the existence of those, or similar, traits within early historic Ireland' (1987: 92-3). The second part of this conclusion is the more grounded and constitutes his more enduring contribution to the dating of the cycle.

As to the modes and composition of the literature itself, Aitchison argues that literature is a sociological phenomenon and must be considered as the particular product of specific social and historical circumstances (93). The key question is whether it plays a passive or active part in the dynamics of society. Failure to study the social and historical context in which it was 'composed' has impaired our understanding of the epic literature. As a result, the problem is that while all scholars appear to agree an oral tradition existed, its relationship with extant written texts has been ignored by most of them (93). Aitchison repairs this omission and, having examined various models of composition and transmission, he concludes that 'the written prose could not simply be regarded as the transcription of oral poetry but rather as literary compositions in their own right'. The character and style of the Ulster cycle sagas give every impression of them having been 'composed in a literary mode' (96). The composition took place within 'the communities of the major monasteries' (99) and 'most probably the late eighth century ... seems the most likely date of composition for the *Táin*' (102).

As the last quotation demonstrates, Aitchison's literary analysis is replete with qualifications. Nevertheless, he asserts with a confidence which the methodology does not sustain that the sources for the *Táin* have an 'ecclesiastical provenance' (102). It would be more scientific to argue that what has been advanced is a hypothesis, even if it is plausible in its own terms.

The difficulty, however, with methodology of the sort used by Aitchison is that the conclusions are never any better than the premises upon which they rest, and if these are suppositions or best guesses in the first place, then the conclusions cannot be rescued from a similar fate even if the intervening argumentation is logically coherent and internally consistent. Aitchison would have been better advised to stick to his formula that the sources of the *Táin* 'appear to attest the monastic context and literary mode of composition and transmission' (102), and then to contrast this argument with Jackson's hypothesis that the background to the Ulster cycle 'appears' to be older than the advent of Christianity and provides us with a 'very dim and fragmentary account' of that Ireland (1964: 5).

Both are hypotheses. Neither has more scientific validity than the other, and both are open to doubt. The only question is, which 'appears' the more likely?

Aitchison landed himself with a problem of some moment when he located the composition of the sagas in the monasteries, because the themes are 'pagan and secular in character' despite later interpolations (1987: 102). Why should the Church propagate such literature? Well, the northern literati were different; their use of the vernacular was unparalleled among the monasteries and the productiveness of the region may be attributed to the *núalitridi*. These were former *filid* recruited into the church and given the role as guardians of their societies' collective memory of the past; they became increasingly active in the study, recording and elaboration of this past (102-3).

One waits for the 'ergo', but none appears. This is a tantalising defect in reasoning as it can only be inferred that the monasteries accommodated both secular and clerical literati and allowed both to flourish in tandem. If so, MacCana's benign model makes a surprising return and McCone's holistic model begins to ship some unholy water.

The pursuit of Jackson then takes a turn into history, whereby the political structure of Ulster for his dating of the *Táin* (1964: 47-8) is held to be untrue in a manner that defies analysis (Aitchison 1987: 103-4). Wisely, Aitchison then resorts to archaeology, where he is on surer ground. Now the geographical focus of the Ulster cycle is Emain Macha, and if it did not exist as a political centre at the alleged time of the *Táin*, then the case for dismissing it as in any way representative of that society would be overwhelming.

Aitchison delivers this knock-out blow by stating that 'excavation ... has demonstrated that Navan Fort was neither a royal residence, nor a fortified settlement, but rather a religious site' (106). Furthermore, not only was it deserted during the period in which the episodes of the Ulster cycle were composed, but it had been abandoned for generations, even centuries before (106). Its employment within the sagas was a physical evocation of the past and, therefore, of ideological importance in transferring some of its status and prestige as a centre of royal authority onto the monastic foundation of Armagh.

All this was done 'during the period of Armagh's claim of primacy from the mid-seventh century' (107). In short, centring the *Táin* on Emain Macha was for the purpose of furthering the political aims of Armagh (107). The relationship between the two was 'a metaphor of the relationship between Christianity and paganism' (108).

This mixture of science and speculation rests on archaeological evidence, for which Mallory is quoted as an authority (Aitchison 1987: 106). Mallory in a later publication (1992a) says that 'the identification of Emain Macha with the modern archaeological site of Navan Fort ... is well accepted'. While it is more likely to have been employed primarily as a ritual rather than a fortified site it is understandable how it might nevertheless be understood as a *dún*.

There is evidence that feasting occurred on site. Mallory also adds that we are not certain of the period when Emain Macha was actually abandoned. He is, however, hesitant about certain features described in the *Táin* but, overall, does not come down on Emain Macha with the absolute certainty of Aitchison (Mallory1992a: 122–3).

Nor does Harbison, who first says there is reason to speculate that Navan Fort may be an Iron Age reincarnation of a much earlier henge monument which may – like Navan Fort itself – have served as a ritual centre for the surrounding countryside. Harbison then notes that the houses excavated there represent, perhaps, the early phases of the *Ulaid* rise to power. As for the site itself: 'it is certainly the most important royal site in the early history of Ulster' (Harbison 1988: 157).

Suffice it to say that the archaeological battle over Emain Macha can only be settled by experts in that field, but, even so, Aitchison's categorical certainty seems overstated. It was inspired, as said earlier, by his ultimate ambition of restoring scientific discipline to his own profession.

Nevertheless, when coupled with criticism drawn from other disciplines, his archaeological exposé did much to undermine Jackson's thesis of the *'Window on the Iron Age'*. Mallory (1992a) developed the archaeological approach further by testing the validity of the *Táin* as an Iron Age or later document against the evidence of archaeology.

But, unlike Aitchison, he warns against the limitations of archaeology, because while there are many portable objects of *La Tène* type in Ireland, 'we are appallingly ignorant of many other aspects of life in the Iron Age' (1992a: 114). Most of the archaeological 'finds' are what he calls 'obscure shadows' that 'cannot be ascribed exclusively to either *La*

Tène or early Christian periods' (114). Now, this does not prevent him from confidently going through a formidable list of material from the *Táin* which is archaeologically identifiable and of then assessing it under various headings (115–51). Nor does it prevent him from drawing conclusions.

These are based on the primary question for archaeologists of whether the 'world' depicted in the *Táin* reflects that of the Iron Age as suggested by Irish tradition or the early medieval period, when the tales were first given written shape. The answer comes in five parts (151–2):

- where good literary evidence is coupled with decisive archaeological evidence the items identified can, in almost all instances, be identified with the early medieval period;
- in a few instances, there seems to be a better fit with Iron Age material;
- a number of literary motifs cannot be regarded as Iron Age inheritances (including chariots composed of exotic materials);
- a number of motifs favour the presumption of an Early Christian date; and
- a few items of Iron Age equipment are unaccountably absent from the *Táin*.

Based on this evidence, 'the material culture of the *Táin* is either demonstrably or probably later than the 4th century ad' (1992a: 152). All the versions that have survived were 'most probably fleshed out (if not created) with the material culture of the early medieval period, probably from the 7th century onwards' (152).

In general, no matter what games one attempts to play with the data, it is impossible to make a convincing case for an Iron Age date for the *Táin* (153). Instead, the case made by Mallory is that the *Táin* is historical fiction, even though to some extent it does hold true as a window on the Iron Age for many items of material culture. The Irish literati attempted to portray a world built out of some genuine recollections of what constituted antiquity, popular folk interpretations of the Irish landscape and literary sources from the Dark Ages (153).

It will be noted that for Mallory, the shift from science to speculation is no less rapid than for Aitchison, and no less sweeping in its scope.

Where he sticks to the scientific arguments, Mallory's scholarship in sifting through the archaeological evidence is far more detailed and comprehensive than that of Aitchison. His approach is methodical, and this allows him to accumulate a formidable body of individual conclusions which, taken in the aggregate, point in the direction of an early Medieval background to the *Táin* in terms of its material culture.

Furthermore, the evidence is so weighty that it cannot be ignored. This can be seen rather dramatically in respect of chariots, which are a central feature of the lifestyle depicted in the *Táin*. The archaeological evidence for chariots in Ireland is extremely small, and most items relating to the chariot have so far remained beyond archaeological retrieval.

Mallory rightly concludes that this fact casts considerable doubt on the notion that the Iron Age Irish employed chariots similar to their neighbours in Britain or Gaul (1992a: 148).

If it were to be taken as a proof, and not just a doubt, then Jackson's 'window' would be reduced to a peep-hole. Mallory makes that leap in reasoning, from doubt to proof, and discovers a quite separate and distinct window which opens on a fictional world that is complex and an amalgam of the past and present. But fictional it is, for the *Táin* is largely devoid of archaeological reality.

In the same publication, Patricia Kelly applies a different form of analysis to the *Táin* (1992: 69–102) by examining its contemporary relevance for the milieu in which it first received its extant form. This technique of exploring contemporary issues by means of narratives set in the past is a new 'paradigm' for a 'new generation of scholars' (72). It allows her to conclude that the most circumstantial anchoring of the *Táin* in time and place and politico-dynastic context is that of Kelleher (1971), who 'tentatively' suggested that it is a political allegory for the struggle between traditional and reforming clergy for control of Armagh in the first quarter of the ninth century (Kelly 1992: 88).

She asks, but does not answer, the question: is the *Táin* a novel? The bigger disappointment is that this type of literary criticism does not lend itself easily to the question of whether or not the substance of the novel is based on history; it is primarily focused on its function within the society in which it was first composed. So great is this pre-occupation that Jackson does not get a mention.

That charge cannot, however, be levelled against Koch (1994). His subject matter was, quite specifically, Jackson's 'window' and is of interest because he is openly sympathetic to his former mentor, despite what he calls 'the now near total destruction of Jackson's case' (1994: 229). In an act of *pietas*, Koch immediately declares his belief that the Ulster cycle preserves 'some traditions from Celtic Europe, in fact, some of the very details for which Jackson made claim' (229). But this is done by proposing a 'sharpened, trimmed, leaner, meaner' version of the 'window' (237). The recollections of ancient Celtic Europe are trimmed down to a list of seven examples, which have essentially pre-Christian and oral sources, including the role of Emain Macha as the chief centre of assembly for the power elite of pagan Celtic Ulster.

Recent archaeological discoveries at Navan Fort tend to confirm rather than refute the proposition that the Ulster tales are an independent witness to the region's later prehistory (229). Koch's version of events is sharpened by jettisoning Jackson's use of the Homeric metaphor both as an epic model for the *Táin* and as an analogy for its composition and transmission. The first is a pervasive error (229), and the second a serious misapplication (230).

The meaner version repairs an error of omission by Jackson, namely a consideration of language in terms of its continuity from prehistoric to early Christian Ireland. This is done by way of an elaborate hypothesis for a language shift from old Celtic to old Irish in the fifth and sixth centuries. The stimulus was the advent of Christianity accompanied by Latin learning, because the new religion temporarily destabilised society and replaced Celtic as a standard learned language with Latin. Whole spheres of oral learning disappeared, and the rest of the vernacular had to be refabricated based on foreign models. It is therefore impossible that a sizeable composition like the *Táin* could have survived verbatim from the fourth century to the seventh.

On the other hand, popular themes, characters, places, episodes and plot devices survived. These were used by Armagh and her daughter houses in the mid-seventh century to represent the pagan Ireland that preceded their founder. In order to enhance Patrick's career as Ireland's apostle, the Armagh propagandists 'had to create a literary realm of pagan Ireland from the retrospective vantage of a triumphant Christianity' (Koch 1994: 232–5).

At the end of this remarkable odyssey, Koch has linked arms with McCone, whom he quotes with approval. It is hard to discern in this hypothesis how it serves to revive Jackson by revising him in a 1990s' version of the 'Window'; rather, it supports McCone's theory of the ruthless reshapers, as Koch himself suggests in a footnote: 'this version of "nativism" is not incompatible with Carney's anti-nativist manifesto' (1994: 237).

Quite simply, Jackson is left without his Homeric analogy, shown to be deficient in his understanding of language change and ignorant of its impact on the oral transmission of epic literature. Not too much remains; even his *La Tène* culture argument is modified. No wonder, then, that Koch believes the 'little book' was so poorly conceived that its only salvageable part is the memorable subtitle (229); all that's left of this particular Cheshire cat is the grin.

Koch's rueful admission of the near total destruction of Jackson's 'window' received further corroboration in *Progress in Medieval Irish Studies* (McCone and Simms, 1996), in which a number of contributors addressed the provenance of the sagas. Ó Cathasaigh, for example (1996: 56–64), deals with early Irish narrative literature and notes that philologists have argued that Ireland preserved much that was Indo-European in origin by virtue of its social institutions, literary tradition and language.

Nevertheless, he emphasises that 'it was the monastic scribes who wrote the earliest of our extant manuscripts ... the monastic scriptoria provided them with a setting for their work' (58–9). Ó Cathasaigh then hardens the case for McCone's thesis of an integrated literary class by a reminder that the Church and the *filid* had reached an accommodation of some kind by the end of sixth century, and by assenting to the proposition that the ecclesiastical literati had by then coalesced with the *filid*.

The significance of this notion, as he calls it, is that it marks a major departure from MacCana's views on 'the circumstances in which early Irish literature was created' (60–1). In a series of rhetorical questions, he disparages the views of MacCana that the monastic scribes confined themselves to pseudo-history and the *filid* were responsible for all of the narrative which can be traced to that period. Hence, Carney is vindicated, despite some overstatement and later recantation, and there can scarcely be any doubt about Ó Cathasaigh's general contention that the sagas as we have them were indeed composed in a Christian literate community (61).

In the same publication, Breatnach, writing on law (Breatnach, 1996a) and analysing the use of the *roscad* style, says it is no guarantee on its own of great antiquity: 'on the contrary, the burden of proof rests on those who would wish to assert that anything written in *roscad* is either earlier than the seventh and eighth centuries, or in any meaningful way represents oral tradition' (Breatnach 1996a: 113).

This is but one further example of McCone's belief that the last bastion of the nativists, i.e. the law tracts, had fallen. Etchingham, also in the same publication, quotes Breatnach as his authority for the argument that the *filid* had been integrated with other learned professionals under ecclesiastical auspices by the Old Irish period (Etchingham 1996: 125).

He expresses his indebtedness to those who recently have 'challenged the traditional perception of the learned professionals' about the contemporary ideology and social fabric of early medieval Ireland. McCone's exposition of the role of biblical models in early Irish literature is noteworthy, and he is held to offer a credible context for 'the persistence of organised paganism in a society the prevalent ideology of which was evidently dominated by the thinking of Christian literati' (*ibid*. 127).

In these circumstances, it is appropriate to leave the last word to McCone himself. His erudite and scholarly analysis of *Echtrae Chonnlai* appeared in 2000, and it allows him to take that saga as a laboratory in which to test the general thesis he advanced ten years earlier. It turns out to be an interesting experiment, with an intriguing set of results. Not unnaturally, there is a reprise of Carney's methodological principle that any text must be viewed a as a whole, and that arbitrary excisions for the purpose of finding correspondence with perceived ideas are unacceptable.

On this solid footing, earlier interpretations, such as by Dillon and MacCana, are rejected as flawed. But there are differences in the treatment of traditional themes – and these differences pose a paradox (2000: 119). In the earliest surviving texts, traditional themes (relating to sovereignty and the otherworld) 'seem to have been subjected to quite ruthless Christian manipulation'. This conclusion is consistent with the ruthless reshaping model. But these same themes appear in some later texts 'in what seems to be a more or less unadulterated form'.

The honesty of these observations is commendable, since they pose a major problem: they are counter-intuitive. One could expect the earlier texts to be unadulterated, being closer to the origins of the subject-matter, and the later texts to be progressively adulterated, being products of a maturing Christianised society. This reversal of the expected, is, indeed, a paradox.

McCone provides a solution based on ideology, which might come perilously close to Carney's 'preconceived notion'. The adulteration of the earlier texts could be explained by the need of the earliest practitioners of this new craft 'to establish their Christian credentials' and so obviate suspicion and disapproval in certain monastic circles (2000: 119).

This would run counter to the argument of the Biblicists, that even by the seventh or eighth century the *filid* had been absorbed into a harmonious literary class. By implication, there is a division between the earliest practitioners of the new craft and certain monastic circles (neither are identified), which requires the practitioners to be more Christian than the Christians themselves, or at least to be as Christian. But when the genre had become established, 'a more permissive attitude may be presumed to have prevailed' (119).

This relaxation in censorship, or thought-control, permitted the monastic production of vernacular narrative with a secular social and/or political orientation. In other words, it was either edited in order to restore or recapture the original in some form, or else it was a new secular genre developed with the assent of the clerical authorities; a hidden Ireland was unveiled or a new Ireland created. Whichever may be true, perhaps they both are, there are strong echoes here of MacCana's 'benign ecumenism'.

McCone's methodological rigour exemplifies the great strength of the biblicist school, but the paradox which he so courageously identified testifies to an analytical weakness yet to be resolved. Unlike the nativist school, which must rely on the scientifically unprovable thesis that an oral tradition existed, the Biblicist School resorts to science and then uses its findings to draw conclusions. But in many cases these conclusions are woven into a complex theory incorporating leaps in reasoning which themselves are unverifiable scientifically.

Aitchison jumps from scientific crag to crag without a thought for the gaps between; Mallory appears more cautious but scales the same heights; Koch winds up in a fantasyland of pre-historic language shift; and McCone is forced to the sort of invention he condemns in others.

None of this is to argue that they are wrong. Rather, the point to be made is that science alone has yet to replace the straw with which even the most prudent Biblicist must still build bricks.

The 'clerical manipulation of ostensibly secular "tradition" for political purposes', weaving all strands of early Irish literature into a 'vast web ... painstakingly and creatively compiled and cultivated' (1990: 255) is the McCone thesis stated at its most dramatic. Certainly the evidence gathered and the manner in which it is organised indicate that it must be taken seriously, and it could well be a new and exciting prism through which to view medieval Ireland.

It most surely accords with many other interpretations of that society, but if advanced as a total, or exclusive, interpretation of the society, eschewing all others, then it must be approached with as much caution as enthusiasm.

Primarily, the methodology employed is that of literary analysis, which of necessity has a narrow focus. The historian, archaeologist and anthropologist would have different views, and might come to different conclusions. Accepting McCone's argument that medieval Ireland was a creative, dynamic society situated in the mainstream of west European civilisation, and was also outward-oriented (as the missionary period proves), there still seems to be persuasive evidence that, at the same time, it retained many distinctive archaic features and was socially conservative. McCone is exasperated by the 'nativists' putting the cart before the horse, as he sees it, and wishes to reverse the order.

What if the cart is before the horse? There still remains a horse and a cart, the two constitute an integral unity, unless unyoked. There seems to be a suggestion that McCone by times wishes to do this, and then again that he does not. Sometimes, enthusiasm for his case carries him too far; at others, common sense leads him to more rounded conclusions.

Should the horse be put before the cart as McCone might in the end wish, it leaves us with a dualist interpretation of Irish medieval society in which the weight of influence is differently distributed from that of the nativists. But both remain, even if in different proportions. It might seem from this that a further challenge presents itself – to reconcile the dichotomy, which so infuriates McCone. Does the double line of descent for the sagas, as identified by Carney (1955: 306) loom as the next great project for Celtic scholarship?

At the end of it all, Jackson's 'window' may be restored for what it was. His modest claim was that the sagas provided a dim and fragmentary picture of the ancient world. Now that some world, or another, existed in Ireland before Christianity is not in dispute. Neither is the effect of Christianity or literacy on that society. Nor is the fact that the sagas were written down in a monastic-based society which, by definition, was Christian. And, finally, there is no dispute that the sagas are fiction, not history, and an amalgam of a pagan past and Christian present.

There is widespread agreement they are great literature. There is enough here for all, nativist and Biblicist.

For Gantz, the sagas, quite apart from their literary value, were a valuable repository of information about the Celtic people (1983: 5) and evidence of a culture of extraordinary vitality and beauty (8). That is no epitaph for Jackson, but a fitting commemoration. For Titley, we should imagine some compromise between the monasteries and the native schools of learning, which had neither gone away nor been totally assimilated (2000: 23).

The tradition of a tradition still lives on. In disputes over the origins of the sagas and the manner of their preservation, the danger is that the uniqueness of early Irish literature can be forgotten and its worth ignored. As Heaney reminds us, there is something to be treasured when it is transcribed and translated, retold and republished, down to our own times (Heaney1994: ix). Jackson would, no doubt, agree.

His 'window' remains of use, even if in need of repair.

Bibliography

Aitchison, N.B. (1987): 'The Ulster cycle: heroic image and historical reality', *Journal of Medieval History* 13, 87-116.

Best, R.I. (1916): 'The Battle of Airtech', *Ériu* 8, 170-86.

Bieler, L. (1966): *Ireland – Harbinger of the Middle Ages*. Oxford University Press.

Binchy, D.A. (1941): *Críth Gablach*, Medieval and Modern Irish Series. Dublin.

Binchy, D.A. (1954): 'Secular Institutions', in M. Dillon (ed.), *Early Irish Society*, 52-65. Dublin.

Binchy, D.A. (1961): 'The Background of Early Irish Literature', *Studia Hibernica* 1, 7-18.

Breatnach, L. (1996): 'Poets and poetry', in K. McCone and K. Simms (eds), *Progress in Medieval Irish studies*, 65-77. Maynooth.

Breatnach, L. (1996a): 'Law', in K. McCone and K. Simms (eds), *Progress in Medieval Irish studies*, 107-21. Maynooth.

Byrne, F.J. (1965): 'The Ireland of St. Columba', *Historical Studies* 5, 37-58.

Byrne, F.J. (1984): 'Introduction', in T. O'Neill, *The Irish hand*: scribes and their manuscripts from the earliest times to the seventeenth century: with an exemplar of Irish scripts. Dublin.

Cahill, T. (1995): *How the Irish Saved Civilisation*. Doubleday, New York.

Carney, J. (1955): *Studies in Irish Literature and History*. Dublin

Carney, J. (1969): 'The deeper level of early Irish literature', *Capuchin Annual*, 160–71.

Carney, J. (1983): 'Early Irish Literature: the State of Research', in G. Mac Eoin, A. Ahlqvist and D. Ó hAodha (eds), *Proceedings of the Sixth International Congress of Celtic Studies*, 113–30. Dublin.

Comyn, D. and Dinneen, P.S. (1902–14): *Foras Feasa ar Éirinn* by Geoffrey Keating, vols 1–4. Irish Texts Society vols. 4, 8, 9, 15 (1902, -08, -08, -14).

De Blácam, A. (1930): *Gaelic Literature Surveyed*. Dublin.

Dillon, M. (1947): 'The Archaism of Irish tradition', *Proceedings of the British Academy* 37, 245–64. (Reprinted 1969, by the American Committee for Irish Studies, Chicago.)

Dillon, M. (1948): *Early Irish literature*. Chicago.

Dillon, M. (1949): 'The Trinity College text of Serglige Con Culainn', *Scottish Gaelic Studies* 6, 139–75.

Dillon, M. (1952): 'The Story of the Finding of Cashel', *Ériu* 16, 61–73.

Dillon, M. (1953): *Serglige Con Culainn*. Dublin.

Dillon, M. (1953a): 'The Wasting Sickness of Cú Chulainn', *Scottish Gaelic Studies* 7, 47–88.

Dillon, M. (1954): *Early Irish Society*. Dublin.

Dillon, M. (1954a): 'The Irish Language', in M. Dillon, Early Irish Society, 7–21. Dublin.

Dillon, M. (1968): *Irish sagas*. Dublin.

Dillon, M. and Chadwick, N. (1967): *The Celtic Realms*. London.

Etchingham, C. (1996) 'Early Medieval Irish history', in K. McCone, and K. Simms, *Progress In Medieval Irish Studies*, 123–53. Maynooth.

Flower, R. (1947): *The Irish Tradition*. Oxford.

Gantz, J. (1981): *Early Irish Myths and Sagas*. Penguin, London.

Greene, D. (1954): 'Early Irish Literature', in M. Dillon, *Early Irish Society*, 22–35. Dublin.

Gwynn, E.J. (1929): 'Senbriathra Fithail', *Revue Celtique* 46, 268–71.

Harbison, P. (1988): *Pre-Christian Ireland: From the First Settlers to the Early Celts*. London.

Heaney, M. (1994): *Over Nine Waves: a Book of Irish Legends*. Faber and Faber, London.

Hughes, K. (1968): 'Introduction', in A.J. Otway-Ruthven, *A History of Medieval Ireland*. London.

Hull, V.E. (1929): 'The Wise Sayings of Flann Fína', *Speculum* 4, 95–102.

Hyde, D. (1899): *A Literary History of Ireland from the Earliest Times to the Present Day*. London.

Ireland, C. (1999): *Old Irish Wisdom attributed to Aldfrith of Northumbria: an Edition of Bríathra Flainn Fhína Maic Ossu* (Medieval and Renaissance texts and studies no. 205). Arizona.

Jackson, K.H. (1964): *The oldest Irish tradition: A window on the Iron Age*. Cambridge.

Joyce, P.W. (1913): *A Social History of Ancient Ireland*. Dublin.

Keating, G. (1902–14): *Foras Feasa ar Éirinn*, see D. Comyn and P.S. Dinneen.

Kelleher, J.V. (1971): 'The *Táin* and The Annals', *Ériu* 22, 107–27.

Kelly, F. (1976): *Audacht Morainn*. Dublin.

Kelly, F. (1988): *A Guide to Early Irish Law*. Dublin.

Kelly, P. (1992): 'The Táin as Literature', in J.P. Mallory, *Aspects of the Táin*, 69–102. Belfast.

Kenney, J.F. (1929): *The Sources for the Early History of Ireland: Ecclesiastical*. New York.

Kinsella, T. (1969): *The Táin*. Dublin.

Koch, J. (1994): 'Windows on the Iron Age 1964–94', *Ulidia* 1, 229–37.

Mac Cana, P. (1979): 'Regnum and Sacerdotium: Notes on Irish tradition', *Proceedings of the British Academy* 65, 443–75.

MacNeill, E. (1921): *Celtic Ireland*. Dublin. (Reprinted 1981, with a new introduction and notes by D. Ó Corráin; Academy Press, Dublin.)

MacNeill, E. (1923): 'Ancient Irish law. The law of status or franchise', *Proceedings of the Royal Irish Academy* 36 C, 265-316.

Mac Niocaill, G. (1975): *The Medieval Irish Annals*. Medieval Irish History Series 3, Dublin.

Mallory, J.P. (1992): Aspects of The Táin. Belfast.

Mallory, J.P. (1992a): 'The World of Cú Chulainn: The Archaeology of TáinBó Cúailnge', in J.P. Mallory, *Aspects of the Táin*, 103-59. Belfast.

Martin, F.X. (1975): 'Introduction', in G. Mac Niocaill, *The Medieval Irish Annals*. Dublin.

McCone, K. (1990): Pagan Past and Christian Present in Early Irish Literature. Maynooth.

McCone, K. (1996): 'Prehistoric, Old and Middle Irish', in K. McCone and K. Simms, (eds) *Progress in Medieval Irish Studies*, 7-53. Maynooth.

McCone, K. (2000): *Ectrae Chonnlai and the Beginnings of Vernacular Narrative Writing in Ireland*: A critical edition with introduction, notes, bibliography and vocabulary. Maynooth.

McCone, K. and Simms, K. (eds) (1996): *Progress in Medieval Irish Studies*. Maynooth.

McManus, D.(1991): *A Guide to Ogam*. Maynooth.

Meyer, K. (1906): 'The Triads of Ireland' (RIA Todd Lecture Series, 13). Dublin.

Meyer, K. (1909): *Tecosca Cormaic: The Instructions of King Cormac Mac Airt* (RIA Todd Lecture Series 15). Dublin.

Murphy, G. (1956): *Early Irish Lyrics*. Oxford.

Nagy, J. (1997): *Conversing With Angels and Ancients*, Cornell University Press.

Ó Cathasaigh, T. (1977): *The Heroic Biography of Cormac Mac Airt*. Dublin Institute for Advanced Studies.

Ó Cathasaigh,T. (1996): 'Early Irish Narrative Literature', in K. McCone, and K. Simms (eds), *Progress in Medieval Irish Studies*, 55–64. Maynooth.

O'Connor, F. (1970): *Kings, Lords, and Commons*. Gill and MacMillan, Dublin.

Ó Corráin, D. (1972): *Ireland Before The Normans*. Four Courts History Classics, Dublin.

O'Flanagan, T. (1808): 'Advice to a Prince by Thaddy Mac Brody', Transactions of the Gaelic Society of Dublin.

O'Rahilly, T.F. (1922): *A Miscellany of Irish Proverbs*. Dublin.

O'Rahilly, T.F. (1946): *Early Irish History and Mythology*. Dublin.

Smith, R.M. (1925): 'On the Briatharthe Cosc Conculaind', Zeitschrift für Celtische Philologie 15, 187–192.

Smith, R.M. (1927): 'The Speculum Principum in early Irish Literature', *Speculum* 2, 411–45.

Smith, R.M. (1928): 'The Senbhriathra Fithail and Related Texts', *Revue Celtique* 45, 1-92.

Smith, R.M. (1928): 'The Alphabet of Cuigne mac Emoin', *Zeitschrift für Celtische Philologie* 17, 45-72.

Smith, R.M. (1929): 'Senbhriathra Fithail', *Revue Celtique* 46, 268-71.

Smith, R.M. (1930): 'Fithal and Flann Fina', *Revue Celtique* 47, 30-38.

Stevenson, J. (1989): 'The beginnings of literacy in Ireland', *Proceedings of the Royal Irish Academy* (C) 89, 127-65.

Stokes, W. and Strachan, J. (1901): *Thesaurus Palaeohibernicus*. Cambridge.

Thurneysen, R. (1917): 'Morands Fürstenspiegel', *Zeitschrift für Celtische Philologie* 11, 56-106.

Thurneysen, R. (1946): *A Grammar of Old Irish*. Dublin.

Titley, A. (2000): *A Pocket History of Gaelic Culture*. O'Brien Press, Dublin.

www.scathánpress.com

www.ingramcontent.com/pod-product-compliance
Lightning Source LLC
Chambersburg PA
CBHW022227010526
44113CB00033B/643